1

DISEQUILIBRIUMS
The Individuals

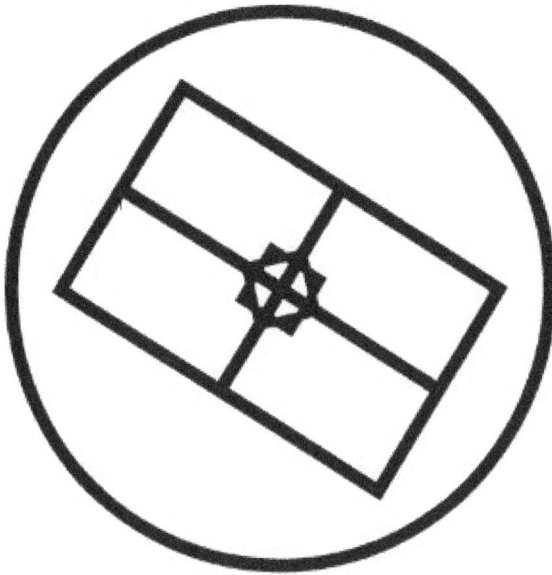

Glen Lapson

Publisher: Fundación ECUUP

This book is part of the project: www.disequilibriums.com/

Writer's Note: Poetic Licence was employed in the use of the word *Disequilibriums* in the title of the novel and within it. According to correct English grammatical usage, the plural form of the word *disequilibrium* is *disequilibria*. The reason for the change is explained in the novel.

For you,
who are always looking for the balance in your town.

In its geographical expansion and lust for power, Rome searched for a place to build a holy city, a place that would meet special conditions, a place that would represent the origin of the Cosmos on earth and a place where the balance between the four elements in nature - earth, water, air and fire - would be achieved.

They found that place in Hispania, and on 23rd December in the year 14 BC they founded a city there. Its people have achieved special characteristics because the balance created by Rome has always been maintained.

But in 2016... that balance is breaking.

PROLOGUE

Friday 23 December 2016.
Time: seconds before dawn

The wind changes direction and the weather vane moves. It has been stationary for an hour. But for a moment, it returns to its normal activity. If it were a person, it would think that it hasn't taken much effort because it normally points in one direction or another. It might ask itself about the purpose of its existence as it has scarcely moved since the end of the year, when it stopped.

Anyone who has travelled there would know that it does not usually remain still.

For most of the time, it points north-west, and the rest of the time it faces south-east. It is really a very active weather vane.

But what the weather vane should be asking itself is what is the real reason for being there?

Remodelled at the beginning of the 20th century, the building has a facade that is a work of art. Above the floors on the same corner at the junction, someone decided to erect a small tower and above it, a weather vane. It is dark in colour with the four points of the compass represented two levels below it. On the first level, there are two perpendicular bars made out of wrought iron pointing in each direction with the corresponding letters forged vertically at each end. On the second level, below, you can see a horizontal circumference in the same colour as the weather vane.

Few citizens in Zaragoza are aware of the existence of this weather vane at the intersection between Don Jaime I Street and the Calle Mayor, which is called 'Espoz' and 'Mina'.

Nor do the people who walk across this intersection look up to watch it today.

It is early. Dawn. There are only two people walking on this corner. A man stops to look to the east at the beautiful tower of

9

the Church of La Magdalena as the first rays of dawn cast their light upon its top.

Suddenly, he lowers his gaze to watch a group of young people running towards him. They seem very excited and are shouting out to each other.

The group quickly reaches the corner. There are three boys and two girls. A boy and a girl are holding hands. Some of them are shouting over each other. The only thing the man can make out that they are discussing is whether it is the exact time that they had to arrive.

They quickly check their watches and agree that it is the correct time. Then, one of the young people takes out a musical instrument and begins to play. The others stop and look around. A few passers-by stop to observe them in silence. Just as the tune comes to an end, there is a burst of light emanating from the centre of the intersection. Suddenly, the wind picks up. As the young man plays the tune, the light gets brighter and the wind grows stronger. The boy looks on as he carries on playing. The others continue to watch the centre. With a mixture of fear and excitement, they begin to shift positions as if preparing themselves for something that is about to happen. The man continues to observe them. He remains motionless, not moving an inch from where he is standing. He stares at the group, arms hanging passively at his side, his body half stooped and his mouth wide open.

When the young man stops playing, in the very space where the streets converge, a dark void opens, with small revolving lights at its centre disappearing in a spiral. Without saying a word to each other, the young people begin to leap one by one, disappearing into the void.

Just at that moment, the young man holding hands with the girl, loses his balance. Their hands come apart. The boy falls as if struck down, hitting his head on the ground and remains motionless on the pavement. The girl can be heard shouting his name, stretching out her arm towards him as she disappears into the nothingness.

Immediately the void closes, the lights disappear and the wind calms.

The man observing the scene and a woman who has approached the area, start shouting and gesticulating for help, and calling for the police as the boy remains lying motionless on the ground. No one else looks at him. No one goes to help him.

If any of the people present had looked up at the building on the corner when the portal had closed, they would have seen that a figure, who had been observing the whole scene from behind the curtains on the 8th floor, had stopped watching and had withdrawn to the interior of the apartment.

CHAPTER 1

Ten days before...

They are rectangular, square, pentagonal, and all linked by some vertex or other and pointed in every direction. Each is a different colour, but with sides of the same thickness, just like the handle of a tennis racket. Each geometric figure is as tall as me. I look all around me, and I see hundreds, thousands, all within a black space. I can't guess where it ends. I leap from one to another, maintaining my balance by holding on to the corners.

Here I come!

I feel myself flying within this infinite space. I'm vibrating, like one of the thousands of water bubbles in a pressure cooker, skipping, exploding, living and dying in less than a microsecond. But they are in a confined space, limited by the hot water below them and the stainless steel lid, preventing them from seeing the sky. I have more freedom than they do. Nothing confines me, although I can't see the sky either. Simply because it isn't there. I am dreaming. How I'm enjoying this!

I see an octagon on my right. Holding on tenaciously to the tip of the triangle from which I am now hanging, I swing myself backwards and, with a full push, release my whole body, launching myself forward to the next destination. I aim for a new target once again.

Oh no! I can't reach it. It's too far. I'm scared. My body is crossing the space, but I'm out of control. I can't believe it. I've miscalculated. I'm getting closer and closer, but not quite close enough.

Aaaahhhh! I'm falling!

Ay! My back hits a square, pointing upwards. The pain! ....but only in my back. I can't feel my legs. I keep falling. My right leg collides with a side of the hexagon below. I can't feel anything. I'm scared. Have I been paralysed?

I continue to fall. My heart's pounding a mile a minute. I can't stop sweating. I can't see anything, ... only lines at the sides and ...darkness.

I can't stand it any longer. I cry out: 'DADDY!'

He doesn't answer. I'm in free fall. My body continues to smash against anything that's there. 'DADDY! DADDY!'

Aaaahhhh! The tears don't even wet my cheeks. I can see them suspended above me, left behind while my body continues hurtling downwards at an uncontrollable speed.

'DADDY! DADDY!'

He isn't here.

It's true. He's no longer here. He hasn't been there for some time.

Suddenly, the classmate I share a desk with, whispered into my ear:

"Sofia, do you understand anything she's said?"

I've been distracted, gazing out the window of the classroom towards the forest opposite with the same thought that I've had for more than a year. I can't control it. As usual, I rub my eyes to calm myself and turn around like a sleepwalker to look at my companion. It is the first time that it's happened in a History class, but this time it's clear, not only to me, that I seem to be bored by the class today.

"No, I don't understand a word," I answer Erik, primarily not to be rude.

On top of not wanting to be rude, not answering the boy you've started going out with and who has decided to sit next to you in class, doesn't seem right.

Erik is tall with short blond hair and very fair skin. He was born in a small town in the north of Sweden. He looks like an athlete. Anyone would think that he is the typical Swedish skier you see on TV, doing a ski jump on New Year's morning, when you get up the day after the party the night before. But no, his only sport was football, and as a result, he has become very close to the other boys in class. He started at our school in September this year, having moved from his country. His parents, also Swedish, work for a renewable energies company which has a branch in Spain. The company chose Zaragoza where there is plenty of wind and sun. Moreover, according to what others have told them, it's better than Madrid or Barcelona because it's a quieter city with good links and they have spoken very warmly of the people.

Two things really attracted me to Erik. The first is his smile. It's no ordinary smile, nor is it forced. Instead, it's natural and, what I value most, in particular, is its sincerity. I don't know if I am strange or what, but I am fed up of people who only smile at you because they've been told that they have to, or they want to get something from you. I prefer they don't smile at me at all. I don't like it when people use it to manipulate you. A smile is something that is part of us and it has to express something we feel. Erik doesn't smile often, but when he does... I love it.

The thing that struck me most about him is his love of music. I reckon that he plays almost every wind instrument I know. I imagine that everyone who lives in those Nordic countries has to have a special hobby, because in winter, if there's no light, they can't get up to much, especially Erik, who used to live in Sundsvall which is further up north from Stockholm. Erik understands all kinds of music. He enjoys them all, as he said: "Not everything fills my soul, but they all touch my heart." Although he likes almost all sorts of music, techno, pop instrumental, soloist and even heavy metal, if he had to choose, he would always opt for jazz. The fact that the saxophone is the first instrument he learned to play when he was small, and has not stopped playing ever since, makes him feel much more in tune with that sort of music.

The only thing that I don't feel comfortable with is the idea of having a boyfriend. I've always had friends who I get on well with, but this is the first time that I have agreed to go out with someone. It isn't that I don't like him. On the contrary. It's more of a social thing. I'm not used to it, and I can't quite understand why, at my age, I should be committing myself to someone.

But all that fades into insignificance, when I look at the History teacher.

How little I like looking at her.

I can still recall the surprise of that first day of school. What a situation it was!

After the first lesson, our tutor, an elderly man dressed in an old-fashioned suit and tie, stayed behind to introduce the new History teacher. The previous teacher, so loved by everyone, retired last summer, after more than 30 years in the classroom. She'd always done the same job: teaching History. I don't know how she could do it - the same thing all the time. I know I can't. Anyway, just as the new teacher came through the door, something happened that's hard to explain.

The boys... it was like a scene from a talent show. As the contestant begins to sing on stage, the camera switches to the celebrities on the judging panel. Their expressions change from total indifference to one full of excitement. This is how it was with the boys. Their mouths dropped open, they put their hands to their faces and some even came close to leaping up and down. My jaw dropped too as we girls all looked knowingly at each other.

The newly appointed History teacher was younger than 30. She was pretty, with long dark hair gathered in a ponytail, which almost reached her waist, and green eyes. She wore clothes which clung to her figure. One of boys in the class stood up and had it not been for the deadly looks from the tutor, the boys might even have burst into applause.

How could she come to give class dressed like that? I thought. Days later, and I don't even know how, we found out that she used to be a professional volleyball player. While she was at university, her team had won the national championship for four years running. She still plays and, what's more, they gave her the job of First Coach of the girls' team in the city.

As a teacher, she must have been good because in every High School she had worked she received excellent recommendations. At the end of the day, we had to accept that it was a done deal. The problem is that, in addition to being lovely, she is very interested in the students. To the delight of the boys in class, she comes in a different outfit everyday. I have never imagined such a young person teaching History. If only she were male and good-looking instead... Well, it is what it is.

Today, she's wearing tight black slacks and a beige wide blouse with sleeves that, when she stretches out her arms to give an explanation, she looks like a person in ancient times, giving a sermon. It's true that the fall of the material under her arms is attractive and highlights what she's explaining. From a distance, I admire the choker-style pendant hanging round her neck on a fine black leather cord, but I can't see the symbol that's on it.

All the same, if I had been distracted looking out the window, Miss *Barbie*, as we girls call her (perhaps to counteract the nickname the boys had given her) was even more so as she explains something without looking once at any of us. How could you teach without looking at your students? How could I like this woman? On the board, she's writing a pile of historical facts and dates about when the ancient Romans invaded the Iberian peninsula.

She must have felt my eyes on her. She turns round, stops and watches me. Obviously, we all have to be looking at her, but I must have been different. I think that it's the first time that she has noticed me. Perhaps she has just read the general boredom in the class reflected on my face. I would have loved to tell her like it is, but I don't. At last, she stops watching me, and with shoulders drooping slightly, as if to release a sigh, she surveys the rest of the class in silence.

She has obviously got the message. Quickly turning around, without saying a word, she switches on the projector and turns off the classroom lights. As she does so, everyone goes quiet and watches her in the darkness. Apart from a small amount of light coming in through the window from the cloudy day outside, the only light in the classroom is the projector light on the wall. I've not stopped watching her. I want to see how she would react.

On the screen, we can see a large map of the Iberian peninsula with the major rivers reflected on it. Still in silence, the teacher points to the map and then, in a loud voice, asks:

"Do you know which was one of the first cities on the Iberian Peninsula to be founded by the Romans?"

In response, some classmates, surprised by Miss Barbie's action, go back to their previously impassive attitude and some of their disappointment show on their faces. They expected something more exciting. I did too. But I'm curious to find out what her next move is.

As neither my classmates nor I answer, the teacher shouts:

"IT IS THIS ONE, THE SAME ONE IN WHICH WE ARE NOW LIVING!"

Erik and I jump. Some look at her quietly while others simply gaze around the room. In fact, Erik watches me and smiles. Although he's only been living in the city for three months, I think that what the teacher is trying to do amuses him.

Miss Barbie draws a large dot on the Ebro River, identifying the position of the city of Zaragoza and writes its name. Then, she turns around and asks the question:

"Do you know why?"

We remain silent, waiting for her to explain. She can see that there are still some people not paying attention. I look at them. They're the usual culprits, as always.

She again turns towards the map and sketches a vertical line crossing the Ebro River in the same place where the city of Zaragoza is positioned on the map. Then, turning to face us again, she explains:

"It is for this reason," she said, pointing at the map, "because it is the only city in which this effect occurs." She

18

pauses, as if waiting for us to guess what she is going to say next. "The horizontal line intersects the vertical line at this point where the Gallego River and the Huerva River merge with the Ebro River."

She has succeeded in getting us interested in what she is saying. It's going well.

In the street, the wind picks up, hissing as it rushes through the window and then slamming it shut. This adds to the air of mystery.

Looking out in the distance, I can see the trees beginning to bend over. The birds have now disappeared. The sky is now heavily overcast. Grey clouds add to the sinister feel of the morning. I turn back to Erik. He is totally engrossed. The light from the projector flickers more brightly than before.

"You see the rivers crossing each other," she continues, "that was a great omen for the Romans. Emperor Augustus, the founder of the city, believed that the goddess of Nature, Cybele, had created the sign of *Cardus* and *Decumanus* – two perpendicular lines, which the Romans used to design their cities. *Cardus* was the main street which ran from north to south, while *Decumanus* ran from east to west. So, from this design, the other streets in the city would be built in regular parallel lines, perpendicular to those built before them."

She stops, stares at us and walks slowly from left to right across the classroom. Today, she hasn't put her hair up in a ponytail. As she moves, her hair sways from side to side. All our eyes are on her now.

"A perfect *Cardus* and *Decumanus* was an expression of the sacred order of the Earth's cosmos for them."

At that moment, she halts in front of a student sitting at the end of the first row on the right. Leaning, with her hands on his table, she turns her face towards the window and we can hear her saying:

"In other words, this was a sacred city for them."

CHAPTER 2

Said like that, it might be interesting, even for the rest of the class. This teacher is good. As my little brother would say: she is 'cool'.

I, on the other hand, have been bored for some time. I can't stop looking at the girl in front of me. Every time I look at her, I feel a lump in my throat. I had begun to feel this way from the first day of class. I don't understand it because we have been together in the same school since primary school, not always in the same class, but in the same school. We shared the same activities, but I had never felt the way I did when I saw her enter my class this year, with her curly hair, worn loose, her open neck and a folder pressed against her body. She walked right past me to sit in front. I don't know whether it was the hair or the clothes that she wore or simply the body of this girl who I shared so many years with at school, but right there and then, she became a woman.

Since that day, I've been thinking about what to say to her, how to explain what I feel for her.

But I can't.

Deep down, I still feel like a child. I carry on playing football with my friends after school. I see her standing at the gate at the exit, chatting with her friends. Occasionally, an older boy would approach the girls and try to join in their conversation. Fortunately, she always went back to her friends. And that calmed my fears.

But one day, my whole world collapsed.

I remember that I was coming to school with my little brother. It is something I have done everyday since my father's death five years earlier, after our mother stopped taking us to school because her new job required her to get into work early every morning. While I was on my way to school, I saw the new boy from Sweden hurrying past me on my left. I liked him. He was friendly, sporty and the girls liked him. When he came alongside, he tapped me on the arm and said:

"David, can I have a word after school?"

I nodded. As I had to come back to collect my little brother from school, we agreed to meet up at the exit gate of the secondary section.

I couldn't have imagined what was going to happen next.

If I'd known, I wouldn't have agreed to meet him later.

When I met this tall blond boy, with white skin and Swedish accent, he told me he'd fallen in love with a girl in class, but didn't know what the custom was in Spain if he wanted to ask her to go out with him. My heart dropped. He'd decided to ask me because I seemed serious and had some experience with girls. How far from the truth he was, I thought to myself. But I'd no time to think more about it when he told me who the girl was.

From that day on, I've tried to avoid looking in her direction, pretty difficult, considering she sits in front of me. In class, we sit in pairs and they put me to sit next to Elsa. So I try to talk to her about topics in class to stop myself glancing at Sofia's table. What is worse, for a whole week now, Erik himself has decided to sit next to Sofia.

I realise I've been distracted. Zaragoza, where I've been living since birth, a sacred city, no less! It's all the more interesting to say the least, because I've never heard about such a thing before.

I've to admit that coming to History class has been worth it this year. She's a great teacher, which is a real surprise. I briefly caught a glimpse of a guy who tried to hit on her the other day at the end of the school day. All he got was a serious rebuff and an eyeful of her boyfriend's muscles when he came to meet her on an enormous motorcycle after school. What an idiot! Imagine at 16, hitting on your teacher who's more than 10 years older than you. Well, each to his own.

I'm just thankful that she hasn't worn high heels like she did on that first day. She made us feel like dwarves, even though she's the shortest player in her volleyball team.

She's still leaning, with her hands on the table at the right-hand corner of the first row. Silently, she observes the surprise on the faces of some students at the idea of a sacred city.

Now, she's grabbed everyone's attention.

"... A place where nature submitted itself to man and perhaps one of the few places where this natural phenomenon truly existed." This was how she ends the history of the city's origins.

She's certainly got my attention. I look at Elsa on my right and she looks back at me. She's Sofia's best friend. How ironic, me sitting next to her. Luckily, I like her. We're always helping each other out in class when one of us doesn't understand something. The dark colour of her skin and her height make her stand out from the rest of the class. With an American father, a former NBA basketball player and a Cuban mother, their daughter is sure to look a little like each of them. She gets her height from her father, and the rest from her mother. From the few times I've seen them together, I can safely say that her character is completely the opposite of her father's. They moved to the city ten years ago when he was hired as coach to the main basketball team. He was kept on for only four years after that, when the club dropped into the Second Division. By that time, the mother had already got herself known as a top class teacher of rhythmic gymnastics in one of the best clubs in the city. So they decided to stay. Her father wasn't short on offers either. He decided to accept a post at the university as an associate lecturer in the Department of Industrial Psychology, using the Doctorate he had obtained in the United States while he was playing basketball.

She continues looking at me. We both shrug our shoulders, in a gesture of puzzlement and, of course, surprise. I know that Elsa loves History. I'm sure that she finds the class very interesting. But the idea of a sacred city sounds a bit far-fetched, and she doesn't believe in fantasy worlds or in imaginary characters. I, on the other hand, don't think it sounded too bad after role-playing with some friends last summer. After all, it was all based on imaginary characters.

"For me, it is a story or a legend," the teacher went on, "but if anyone succeeded in proving it to be true, that would be amazing. What is certain is that there is more to tell." She stops and looks at us.

There's a long silence in the classroom, as we wait for her to continue her explanation. She points to the drawn map and proceeds with the explanation:

"The Romans knew the large river which ran from the west to the east: the Ebro. In fact, by now, you are probably asking yourselves why the Iberian Peninsula carries the name that is derived from the river passing through our city."

Then, she drops her pen. Bending over to pick it up, she creates a moment of sensation in class ... at least among the boys. The girls, on the other hand, focus the map.

"For them, it was the river coming from the west, from the world of the dead, of darkness, of twilight..."

I realise that I'm staring at her. It's been a while since something like that has happened to me, at least for reasons other than her looks. Surreptitiously, I watch my classmates. I don't want them to see me doing it. The fact is I do it often, but I don't want them to think that I am a voyeur. It's basically curiosity or so I tell myself when I watch them. This time, I see that they're all looking at the map intently and listening attentively to the teacher.

"...And it was the river that flowed toward the east, where the sun, the light rose ... towards Rome. It was the river which suddenly converged with two others: one running from the north, from *Gallia* (hence its name: the Gallego) and the other, the Huerva, bringing waters from the south."

The teacher is silent as she points out the rivers on the map. She then continues:

"The direction of the water's flow was regarded as the transport or as a vehicle of information from its source. In other words, the river that carried water from the North, from the Polar Star, brought water from the Cosmos, from knowledge itself."

Suddenly, Elsa commented in a low voice:

"In other words, people from the north are smarter than us."

From the ensuing silence, it appears that everyone in the class has heard her. With hoots of laughter coming from all sides, Elsa blushes and the teacher addresses her point:

"The truth is that I don't know how to respond to that," she smiles, "because if I tell you about the river from the south, I don't know what conclusion you are going to come to."

There's a slight pause while she smoothes her hair with her hands. Then she carries on:

"Because the one from the south, if we accept your interpretation, carried with it information from the Earth, from the material underworld, from the serpent or the dragon up to the north."

Now, I don't know where to look. I can see Elsa beginning to feel uncomfortable. She glances at me, as if to say that this is all beginning to sound like nonsense. But like me, everyone continues to listen. After all, it's a fact that these rivers do exist. I notice that the class is totally silent.

"We might conclude that the city of Caesar Augustus was designed to be the centre of the Roman Order. As a consequence, they looked upon it as a sacred city, designing it to be a representation on Earth of a world ordained by the gods."

She walks silently towards the window. Outside, the day looks as dark as night. The wind picks up. Through the window, we can see the clouds have all turned almost black. We all know that they are a prelude to a storm.

Suddenly a bolt of lightning in the distance startles us. We can hear gasps from the girls. Then, there's total silence in the classroom. No one's looking at the screen. Without taking her eyes off the window, the teacher says in a loud voice:

"Do you know how this link between the heavens and the earth was created?"

I look at the others. Nobody responds, including me. There's only silence. It's the first time that something like this has happened in a History class. It's the first time in the whole year that the teacher has been able to hold everyone's attention with an explanation. She turns back to the map. All eyes follow her, like spectators at a tennis match. No one says a word.

The teacher answers her own question:

"By geometry."

She stops and looks at us again.

"In this way, the Roman town of Caesaraugusta was geometrically designed, using knowledge held only by the priests. It was assumed that they were the only ones who understood the true depths of the mystery of life."

Unabashed, I look at Sofia. I know all too well that she will be enjoying this. And so she is. She's shifting in her seat and sitting upright at her desk to listen more intently.

"For this reason, custom prescribed a foundation ritual to create the city. What happened is that the priests drew perpendicular axes between each point on the earth, the *Cardus* and the *Decumanus*. To do so, they used two oxen to pull a plough to mark the perimeter of the city. The Earth represented the material world: the feminine form impregnated by the plough which, in turn, was the symbol of masculine energy, both of them being sacred ..."

She waits for a moment and surveys her audience.

"Hence, they gave the city a sacred character. They understood that it was a place of Order or, in other words, they created a City of Harmony because a balance had been created by combining these two energies."

The teacher stops for moment and contemplates the look of surprise on our faces. I glance at the rest. We're all the same. She puts up a large plan of the old city and draws two thick

25

lines: one along Don Jaime I Street from the Ebro River to Coso Street, and the other from the Plaza of La Magdalena along Calle Mayor, Espoz, Mina and Manifestación Streets, to end at Caesar Augustus Avenue.

She turns and says, pointing at the two thick lines she has drawn:

"Behold: the *Cardus* and the *Decumanus* of Zaragoza."

I recall someone else mentioning this earlier at some point in my life. I'd never given it any importance. Now, it seems that it is. Elsa sits with her mouth wide open. I look at Sofia again. She's the only one in the class not looking at the board. Instead she's busy, scribbling something down on a sheet of paper.

But, at that point, something else is happening.

I don't know what it is.

The teacher lifts her right hand to her ear. Her expression quickly changes into one of pain. She has to support herself on the table with her other hand. She looks dizzy. She starts bending her head forward and pursing her lips. What's happening to her? She's falling.

Good God! She literally collapses on the table, holding onto the edge of the desk with her left hand in order not to fall to the ground. There's shouting in the classroom. Suddenly, it's chaos.

The students in the first row get up and run to her assistance.

By then, we can see that her hair's stained with a streak of red, from the blood trickling from her right ear. With her fingers, she tries to stop the flow. With her head resting on the table, she looks at us helplessly, as if trying to ask what's going on.

CHAPTER 3

Thursday 15 December 2016
Time: 8:45 am

Sofia

I've seen couples walking along the street hand in hand or with the boy's arm over the girl's shoulders.

But today I look upon it differently. I look upon it differently because I am one of those couples. We've been walking around the city for a while and Erik has just put his arm on my shoulder. We've just passed Plaza Paraíso, walking along Paseo Constitución towards Plaza de los Sitios, and we've begun to cross the street along with other people.

I feel uncomfortable, but I can't tell him as it's the first time that he's done it. He seems to like it, or so it appears when I glance at him. As other couples behave like this, I prefer to let it be, and I don't want to be any different today, at least not for the moment. But I'm different in many ways, as for instance how to be with boys, especially since this is the first time I've gone out with one.

In any case, it's good that he's putting his arm around me because it's cold. It's a typical winter's day in Zaragoza with a cold freezing wind. Although it's sunny, the wind chill factor makes it feel as if it's below zero. This city's strange. 'Anyone who can stand the cold winter and afterwards the suffocating heat of summer, can live anywhere in the world!' I remember the woman who sold bread near our house when I was little saying that to me when I was small.

The time on his watch is 8:45. So, we're probably a few minutes early. I look up at Erik's face. I need to look up because he's a head taller than I, although we're the same age. He's not recognised that the scarf around his neck is touching my face. The wind's so strong that his scarf's flapping against my face. Very gently, I slip his arm from my shoulder.

27

We continue walking.

"Have I offended you?"

I stop in the middle of the intersection on Juan Bruil Street. I wasn't expecting to hear Erik saying those words. What's he referring to? What's he talking about? I've not said or done anything to upset him. Or so I think.

"Why do you say that?"

We're standing with his eyes locked on mine, but I can't guess what he's thinking. I look around at the people walking very briskly along the walkway. There are groups of boys of our age walking from both directions. Everyone here is watching us and I don't know what he's going to say.

I grab his arm and we head towards the Juan Bruil Street, where it would be more discreet. At the end of the street, from a distance, I can see all the people walking along Paseo Independencia and, behind me, at the other end of the street, those I've just seen along Paseo Constitución, but in this little lane, there's no one.

"Don't you like me?" Erik stops me on the pavement and we stand with our eyes locked on each other.

What's he getting at? What's wrong with him?

"Yes, I do." I try to make him see that I'm frowning.

He passes his right hand across his face as if he's nervous.

"It's that..." He stops.

I can't speak.

"You sometimes seem so cold with me. I come from another country and perhaps with the cultural difference we're not getting along. Perhaps I'm not behaving as I should..."

I can't take my eyes off him. I'm totally dumbfounded because I've not expected anything like this. And what can I say to him now?

"... I like you very much," Erik continues, "and since we've started going out together, I like you more and more each day."

"I like you too," I respond, watching him closely, "I love being with you..."

28

It's true, but it doesn't come out naturally. He's great guy, with a big heart and besides, he's very good-looking, but I want to get to know him better. I suppose the problem is me because I've never been able to express my feelings.

"Well, it doesn't show," he quickly interrupts me.

"Why do you say that?"

He continues looking at me. He must have realised that he's annoyed me.

"Sorry," he starts saying. "It is just that ...I see other couples and they talk more than we do, they hold hands, and they are more affectionate to each other. But we..."

I put my finger on his lips, with the only sign possible.

My smile makes him relax. I tiptoe and put my arms around his neck. He looks at me from his height and puts his arms around my back.

How good he smells. I've never asked him what cologne he uses because it would seem superficial, but I know that they don't sell it in this city. Well, at least none of the adults or young men I know use it. His slim figure and his short blond hair look more incredible than ever because of the olive green high-necked jumper he's wearing. He's wearing jeans, but he's not given me any opportunity to see him coming as his face comes close to mine. He's taken the initiative and I like that. He tilts his head to the left and I towards mine. As he comes closer, our lips meet. I feel his strong hands caress me as they move up and down my back. My whole body clings to his. He must have felt the unavoidable response from every part of my body which is in contact with his, in the same way that I'm aware of those he can't control. I like it. I'm completely lost in these sensations. I don't know where I am. It's as if I'm floating on the clouds and I don't want it to end. How I like Erik! I feel him very close. It isn't just the kiss. It's something more.

"Excuse us."

The voices of the couple who've just left the hotel with a baby's pram make me blush and I immediately move away from Erik. We've taken up the small pavement and they can't get past.

"Sorry," we apologise together, smiling at each other amid conspiratorial looks.

We remain standing as the couple walk away in the distance towards the Paseo Constitución. Just as they're turning right and before disappearing round the corner, the man looks back and, with a small smile, gives us a wink.

We gaze at each other again, we smile and hold hands.

"Erik, I like you a lot and I assure you that there's no problem. The problem is me. As I told you the first time we went out, you're the first boy who I've ever gone out with. Perhaps it is I who do not know how to behave."

It's impossible to explain to him that I was not like this a year before. I was more chatty with everyone and more friendly. I loved being surrounded by people to chat and chat and chat. But since my father's disappearance, everything's changed. I'm not the same.

I tiptoe and give him a quick, unexpected kiss.

"I am sure that we're going to spend more time together with this History project and we'll have a great time."

We hold hands, with our fingers intertwined, and I move a little away from him to avoid his flapping scarf.

He releases my hand, puts his right arm around my shoulders and, as if he guessed what led up to this moment, he wraps his scarf around us both. That's better. I like it.

We continue walking towards our destination along Tomás Castellano Street.

As we're about to enter the Church of Santa Engracia, I break the silence:

"What do you think of what happened to the History teacher?"

My question takes him unawares, as if he thought I wanted to change the conversation.

"Very strange." He glances at me as we continue walking. "I've never seen anything like it. I hope it's nothing serious."

His words are lost on me because I'm distracted by a woman who's entering the church. She loses her balance and would have fallen were it not for her friends who held her. She raises her hand to her right ear and, as she removes it to watch her palm through her magnifying glasses, I can see a red colour staining it.

CHAPTER 4

Thursday 15 December 2016
Time: 8:55 am

David

As luck would have it, we arrive 10 minutes earlier than the time we arranged to meet up with Sofia and Erik. Elsa spots me and smiles. I smile back. As we wait, we sit down on one of the benches in the Plaza de los Sitios. Knowing her preference for being different, I follow her example and sit on the backrest of the bench with my feet on the seat.

It's cold. We're protected from the worst of it by our coats, but she's still constantly re-wrapping her scarf around her neck.

I stop watching her and turn my attention to stare down Joaquín Costa Street in the distance to see if they're coming. I can sense Elsa looking at me.

I can't help thinking about the conversation I had with my mother the day before.

It was seven in the evening. In the middle of the department store, she told me:

"Thank you!"

I was so surprised that I stared at her with my eyes wide open – so much so that she too looked startled.

We'd been in the Children's Clothes department for around a quarter of an hour while she looked for a pair of trousers for me. It was the worst time of the year to buy anything that was necessary. We found ourselves surrounded by hundreds of people who were there simply because it was close to Christmas. If only they knew how much I wanted to get away from all the stereotypes and customs! Anyway, even though I wanted to escape, it had become impossible when my mother had told me earlier that evening that I had nothing to wear for the following day.

32

She had told me 30 seconds after showing me the bleach stains on the jeans that I had been wearing that day in class. She wasn't interested in my detailed explanation about how the bottle of sodium hypochlorite had fallen accidentally in the Chemistry lab. She simply looked at me and told me that I didn't have any more trousers.

"Why are you thanking me?" I asked, looking at her.

For a second, there was a flush of excitement or even, joy on her face when she spoke. Since the death of my father, she had sunk into a state of loneliness and sadness, which made my brother and me try to animate her. So I had to prolong the moment for as long as possible.

"For coming with me."

"I don't understand," I replied as I continued watching her happy expression.

"Look around you."

And so I did. The store was packed with people, as it always was at that time of year. By the look on my face, she must have realised that I didn't understand what she was talking about.

"Thank you for letting me accompany you," she said. "While you were looking for trousers, I noticed that no other young man had come with his mother. Almost all of them were with a friend or in a group."

I hadn't even noticed. But as I studied the scene more closely, I realised that she was right. I remembered that it was almost a year since I had not wanted her along. It was true. But for some reason I couldn't remember, I had asked her please to come with me. I must have told her that I needed her opinion as a woman. Why did I tell her that? I still had no idea. The problem was that I didn't know what to say after that.

My mother looked at me closely for a moment. I enjoyed this look of happiness radiating from her.

"Are you OK?" she asked suddenly. "Are you feeling alright?"

I nodded as I looked at a navy blue pair of trousers in my size.

"Is it about what happened to your teacher?" my mother continued.

I had talked about it with her and my brother the night before at dinner. I think I had included the detail about the blood. I must have been too descriptive because my little brother told me the following morning that he was too afraid to sleep.

"No," I answered.

I could sense her eyes pinned on me. I turned and looked at her.

"Is it because of a girl?"

What was she doing now? I thought. A mother wasn't supposed to be asking her 16-year old son *that*. That's private. What's more, she wasn't supposed to know about it. I hadn't given her the slightest reason to suspect it. That was my business and mine alone.

But as I hadn't answered her immediately, she carried on:

"Don't worry. It's normal. What is important is that you tell her as soon as possible so that you can get to know each other better..."

She fell silent for a moment. I took advantage of her silence to move to another display area and began to look at some jeans, hoping that the moment would pass. I hated that she was interfering in my personal life, but I loved her a lot and with everything she had been through, I felt incapable of doing anything that would make her suffer (or so I thought). She moved closer to where I was standing and continued:

"Furthermore, that black girl is very pretty and she seems a very good person."

I could stand it no longer and I jumped.

"MUM! The black girl that you are talking about," I continued to raise my voice, "has a name. Her name is Elsa and I share a desk with her in class. As you say, she is very nice and a good friend. And nothing more! DON'T INTERFERE IN MY PERSONAL LIFE AGAIN!"

34

I knew at once that I would never regret anything so much as I did my action then.

The little spark of happiness that I had detected minutes before vanished. She turned pale. She looked straight ahead. She did not want to know how many people on the floor in the department shop at the moment had heard a 16-year old boy shout at his mother. She simply looked at me, and with one of the saddest looks that I had ever seen on my mother, except for the day they told her that her husband had died in a car accident, she told me:

"Sorry. I will not do it again."

That night, over dinner, even with my brother present, I couldn't stop apologising. Even though she repeated many times that it didn't matter and that all was forgotten, I have never seen that spark again. It would be a burden that I would have to carry a long time.

I don't know what made me feel worse: what she thought about my taste in girls or that I had a relationship with a girl who wasn't my type.

And here I am, sitting with her on the bench. I have to admit that she's a great person and a real looker. She's the kind of girl who I would recommend to my best friend to go out with. But my heart has been captured many months ago, at a point of no return, far from Elsa.

"Look, here they come!"

Elsa's words bring me back to the present. Following her finger, pointing in the direction of the Church of Santa Engracia, I see Sofia and Erik approaching in the distance.

Erik has his arm draped around Sofia's shoulders.

CHAPTER 5

Thursday 15 December 2016
Time: 9:00 am

Sofia

Erik's arm has not been on my shoulder for more than five minutes when, in the distance, as we are going down Joaquín Costa Street towards Plaza de los Sitios, we spot the others who we've agreed to meet at the entrance of the Provincial Museum.

I detach myself quickly from Erik. This is something that we can't do. It's one thing to hold hands among strangers, and another to do it in front of your mates, above all, in front of David, who I've known for a long time. In recent months, he's been behaving a little strangely towards me. I don't know what's happened, although I'm not bothered. I've too many problems of my own.

Samuel, the fifth member of our group isn't able to come on the visit we've planned for today. He sent me a text message, telling me that he's at home, down with a fever. What a nuisance! He's a very special person. In class, not everyone accepts him, but I really like working with him. I hope that he can make it for the next visit we organise for the work we're doing together.

"It's a strange day!" Erik says in his Swedish accent as we approach.

With their feet up on the seat, Elsa and David are waiting for us on the bench in the plaza where we've agreed to meet.

"A typical *cierzo* day as usual, at this time of year!" David remarks in a hostile tone. I even reproach him with a look.

Erik and I join them on the bench, as I glance at David because of his unfortunate comment.

"Do you know how the History teacher is?" Elsa asks as we sit down.

Nobody answers.

Remembering what happened in class the previous Tuesday is unpleasant. After she began to bleed through her ear, they helped her to a seat. She wiped her face with a handkerchief that the boy with curly hair in the front row had given her. When she checked that she was no longer bleeding, she told us that she was going to put us in teams of five and that each team had to take a sheet from her desk with the instructions she had prepared at home.

No one said a word. We all just stared at her.

"This morning my mother called the school and they told her that she was better, but she was at home." David surprises us all with his comment.

We were forced to leave the classroom as soon as the bell rang for the next class. As we were leaving, the classmate who had gone to tell the Headteacher had returned, accompanied by the school nurse.

The next thing we learned yesterday from the tutor who was with us was that the teacher had stayed home. He told us that she was dizzy and could not walk, but the doctor who treated her said that it would pass in a couple of days and we would soon have her back in class again.

We were all happy when we heard the news, although I don't think any of us can easily forget the colour of the blood. The tutor read out her instructions and the make-up of the groups the teacher had given him over the phone so that we could all be organised to start the new project.

"Why has the teacher chosen Samuel to do the project with us?" Elsa asks, David's response comes immediately:

"Because she likes us."

That have us all laughing for a bit. He's back to being *Mr Affable*, as usual. In truth, the work Miss Barbie has set us doesn't look much like a present. On reflection, I decide that with everything that's happened, it's probably best to stop calling her that. After the explanation the day before on *Cardus*, *Decumanus* and the Roman history of the city, her instructions force us to work in groups of five to prepare a 30-

37

page project. It has to be a well-documented presentation to the rest of the class in only 20 minutes. We have to find out all that we can about the intersection of the *Cardus* and *Decumanus*.

She's succeeded in raising our interest during the lesson, but from that to do such a project is a totally different matter altogether.

"I have to say," Elsa starts saying, "that deep down I like this topic. In the beginning, all this talk about a sacred city of ancient Rome sounded stupid, but what she said afterwards got me going. Imagine if this were all true and they really did build a sacred city."

"I don't really believe in this sort of thing," I remark. "But, at the same time, I have to admit that what attracted my attention the day before yesterday was the geometry."

I sense a smile on David's face. However, I don't think it's because he thinks my comment is humorous.

"I asked at home last night," Erik mentions, staring vacantly at the plaza, "and no one in my family knew anything about the Romans or sacred cities. However, my father said he knew about the *Cardus* and *Decumanus*. The truth is, I felt kind of strange talking about a sacred city."

We're still sitting on the bench in front of the Provincial Museum, waiting for it to open. My dad had brought us to see every monument in the city, but on the two occasions we had come to this one, it was closed. I recall that he told us that it's an old building in a neo-Renaissance style, built for the 1908 Hispano-French Exposition to commemorate the 100th anniversary of a historical event in the city, the first Siege of Zaragoza. Located at one end of the Plaza de los Sitios where we're waiting, it's very well laid-out for visits, according to my father.

The plaza, rectangular in shape, is a space with many trees, children's games and a monument in the centre. Moreover, with its well-placed benches, you have a good view of everything happening around you.

You can say that the plaza has come alive. Every morning, you can see elderly people taking a stroll in the plaza or enjoying a rest on the benches. In the afternoon, it becomes very lively with mums and dads letting their small children play on the swings; and at the end of the evening, and mainly at the weekend, it's people of our own age taking up various spaces, meeting up to hang out. It's become the thing to do. Almost every Saturday afternoon, we come here to do something completely different from the reason we are here this morning. If trees could talk, I'd ask them about the many things they could tell us!

As I look at the children's swings, now empty because it's a school day, I remember that before the birth of my little sister, my mum used to bring my brother and me to play there.

I have goose bumps thinking about the first time when she taught me how to play on the swings. She and I used to come alone. In the beginning, I thought it was impossible. But, I don't know whether it was my effort and persistence or my mum's patience that made me, on that first day, learn to push myself on my own and 'fly' in the swing, as we used to say. At the end of that day, I was rising almost above the cross bar. It looked like it was going to go over. It was exciting. My mother looked on at me with pride, unlike other mothers who were shrieking hysterically at their children not to go so high.

I felt powerful, high above everything and everyone.

In particular, because I was such a small girl, I had looked forward to the day when I wouldn't have to tilt my head so far back to talk to adults. Now, that day has come. I have grown up. I am already a woman. And here I am in the same spot where I had learnt... only years later.

What I remember most about that day is the exact moment when I brought the swing to a stop.

My mum came up to me and gave me a big hug of congratulations, and suddenly, we were spinning around in a whirl.

A few metres behind us, a man applauded us drawing the attention of several parents to us. I remember looking into my mother's eyes. We were speechless.

"Very good, very good!" the man applauded as he approached the swings.

I imagine that he wasn't so old but, at that time, I thought that he was over 80. Of average height and white-haired, he was well-wrapped against the winter cold by a type of white cape which revealed baggy, white trousers, under which you could see that he was wearing black boots. What struck me most about him was his face. He had sun-weathered skin, sunken cheeks, and a perfectly clean-shaven face, offsetting his intensely bright blue eyes. This gave him an unusual look. His face appeared full of life. He regarded me gently but, at the same time, there seemed to be a positive force emanating from his eyes. I must have been mesmerised by them because I stared into them for some time without saying anything. When I finally realised how passive I had become, without breaking my gaze, I answered him:

"Thank you!"

He came closer to us, and bending down towards me, he said:

"I was not referring to you, little one." He pointed to my mother who was watching us and contemplating the moment. "I was referring to her."

My mum became a little more serious, as if distant, and uncomfortable. She grabbed me, put her arms around me and drew me towards her. I had always liked when I felt protected by her. I loved whenever something like this happened because, on account of her many business trips, the moments we spent together were quite infrequent at the time.

"Forgive me, madam." The man spoke again, stepping back a little. "I did not want to worry you. But I could not help congratulating you. What I have just witnessed here this afternoon is a great example of perseverance, encouragement and bravery."

I noticed that my mother had relaxed a little more.

"Thank you," she began, "I am proud of my daughter."

"I am sure of it. What is more, she should be proud of her mother because it is you who have communicated those values to her. I wonder who could have transmitted them to you."

"What do you mean?" asked my mother a little more seriously.

"Look," he moved away from where we were standing towards the statue at the centre of the plaza. "I come here on many an afternoon to meditate on this monument here in the Plaza Los Sitios. The total valour demonstrated by this city's inhabitants when they confronted the French army in 1808, preventing them from entering the city, received international acclaim for its bravery and perseverance. It was a pity that so many people died. Eventually, the city had to surrender."

He turned back to the monument and continued:

"Every citizen fought against their attackers; groups of women came out of their homes brandishing utensils as battle weapons; many men were suddenly and almost seamlessly transformed from farmers to soldiers. The whole episode stood out for their commitment to a common purpose."

Although I had visited this plaza dozens of times, I had never really given the monument a proper look. Although I was still young, the man's words made me more interested in it.

"Observe!" He pointed to an area where you could see a woman with a canon. "That is Agustina Zaragoza, on her own, firing the artillery cut off when the gunners, who were aiming it, were hit by a shell."

Until then, I had never heard the story of this woman's bravery.

He went on describing many events in the battle depicted in the monument, covering details that I cannot recall. What the man seemed to be saying was part of the story of war that I wouldn't normally pay much attention to; but this was something about my city and the way he talked about it so passionately made you feel as if he had been there to witness it all.

"Where do you think she and all the people of Zaragoza got that bravery and strength from?"

He was silent for a moment.

"Your mother," he turned once more to look at me, "has it and without your realising it, she has passed it on to you."

As he said it, I felt a shiver pass through me.

It wasn't just a question. It was something more. There was something mysterious in his words that I didn't understand at the time, nor even to this day.

My mother abandoned the defensive posture she had at the start of the conversation. I now saw that she too was captivated by what the old man might say next.

"There is something in this sculpture, which few people have considered and within which lies the true mystery of the image."

He moved to the right and pointed to the section where you could see some men trying to support something looking like a wall with poles or, you might even say, with their own bodies.

"See, these men died trying to protect the gates against enemy invasion. Specifically, the gates of San Lázaro and Santa Isabel's convents."

He looked at each of us in silence for a few seconds, and then continued:

"It was an impossible task as, on the other side, there were horses pushing against them. But there they stood, remaining there to the very last until they were finally crushed. Few people have considered their real reason for protecting those gates, which cost them their lives. Some believe that it was simply because they kept their weapons there..."

He left the sentence unfinished.

Next, holding my mother's gaze, he added:

"I am sure that someone will be able to discover the truth."

I remember the moment clearly and I still can't decide whether it was a challenge or … a command. His tone was serious.

He turned back towards us and, with a smile that I shall never forget, he said:

"The day when all that is depicted in this statue is lost, the city will fall." He kept silent for a few seconds, observing my mother closely. "Fortunately, little girl," he said as he turned his head gently towards me, "there are people like your mother."

I remember that he put something into my mother's hand. It was small, so small that I could not see what it was when she closed her fist around it. I still can't understand why he explained all this to me on that day, or the two or three occasions later when I recalled that event.

The man then turned and walked away in the direction towards Zurita Street. He was erect as he walked away with a firm stride. Perhaps it is the mistaken impression of a small girl, but if it were not for the fact that he was an elderly man, I would have sworn that it was the stride of a soldier.

And here I am again, gazing at the same men in the sculpture, trying to hold up that door, at the cost of their lives. Every time I walk through the plaza, I look at those men. What were they trying to protect? What made them do it?

I am roused from my thoughts when Elsa points out that the museum is about to open. Nobody moves. Inadvertently, Erik brushes against my hand. I glance around. As he makes a gesture to apologise, I look him in the eye and smile, furtively caressing his hand with my fingers. For a moment, we remain gazing at each other with our fingers intertwined.

This detail is not lost on David as he watches us.

With a look of disgust, he looks away, gets up from the bench and walks across the street towards the museum.

Suddenly, there's a cry of pain.

"Oh my God!" David's shouting.

"What's wrong?" Erik reacts quickly, immediately moving away from me and rushing towards David.

As we all turn towards David, a few metres in front of us, we see two people lying dazed on the ground, with their hands clutching their ears.

We stare at them, dumbstruck. One is an elegantly dressed elderly lady and the other, a young man, about 20 years old who, I guess, works on the construction site nearby. My eyes scan the entire plaza and, at the entrance of the Provincial Museum, I notice several more people on the ground at different points.

Apart from the lady at the entrance of the church of Santa Engracia while we were walking to the meeting point, there are some young people who, likewise, are sprawled on the grass in the plaza. Near the swings, a tramp is also lying stunned on a bench. I didn't notice any of this before. However, in that short period alone, I have already counted at least seven people lying prostrate in various parts of the plaza. The last two figures I can make out on the corner nearest the Red Cross building, near the parked cars, are two men dressed in suits and ties.

However, that isn't what is so surprising.

What astonishes me is that no one else seems to notice. They walk on by, without even looking at the people on the ground.

By this time, the plaza is quite crowded. There's a large group of people going to Government offices on the corner adjoining the museum.

None of them seem taken aback or, indeed, take the slightest notice of the bodies collapsed on the ground.

Without a murmur, we follow them, walking towards the museum entrance.

For some reason, I glance back at the sculpture in the centre of the plaza, at the heroic figures protecting the gates of the convent.

At that precise moment, the last words of that elderly man, uttered so many years earlier, reverberate in my mind: the city will fall.

CHAPTER 6

Thursday 15 December 2016
Time: 10:00 am

David

The first thing that strikes you when you enter the Provincial Museum is the enormous hall. It is more than five metres high, lined by tall columns with capitals of the ancient kind which, they told us in class, were decorated with a species of leaves.

"Corinthian, David. Corinthian capitals." That was always my mother's response after I asked the same old question whenever I accompanied her.

I never have time to study them because a very kind person on your left would ask if you needed help. Normally, that same person would invite you to go to the left again. There, you would find a counter with a lady primed to give you information about the museum or to guide you to the section you wanted to see. Shelves full of leaflets and books encourage you to find out more before your visit.

This scenario is repeated today.

I know it so well from the many times I've come before with my school or with my mum.

Although I am the first to cross the street to enter the museum, it's Sofia who takes the lead, overtaking me and urging us to follow her. She doesn't wait for us before going in herself. As she's always telling us, she doesn't like wasting time. She leads us straight to the information desk to ask where exactly the Ancient Rome exhibition is.

I wish I was as decisive as her. But I prefer to mull over things before doing anything. As I watch her striding on ahead, I try to guess what she is thinking about, as she turns her head from side to side as tourists do without fully understanding what they are looking at. She probably thinks she's wasting

46

time. She always says the same thing. I can imagine the words running though her head as if I were in her mind. She's an unstoppable force.

I'll never forget when she told me that meditation isn't her thing. She prefers action even though her mother insisted that one day she will need it. She recounted that her mother had told her: "You are living through a very beautiful period now as you are young, but when you grow up and life becomes intense, you will need to put aside some time for relaxing and reflecting." On the day she told me this, we were alone. I could scarcely believe it. She allowed me to walk home with her after school. Everything she did thrilled me – how she walked, how she touched her hair, her smile, the shape of her mouth... We were standing waiting for the lights to change, for the cars to stop to let us cross. She began to talk about herself and her childhood. I couldn't remember how many times the lights changed before we finally moved. It was clearly a sign that she wanted to be with me. I could sense how close she was. The scent of her perfume intoxicated me and made me want to move even closer.

Her long, red curls were flowing in the strong wind that was blowing that day. Her beautiful green eyes stared far into the distance as she spoke, preventing me from meeting her gaze and searching her eyes for that same distant place which was allowing her to open up to me as she had never done before. I couldn't stop staring at her. She was so beautiful. I would have put my arms around her and kissed her there and then in front of all these people, if it hadn't been for the fact I didn't know how she would react.

Suddenly, I realised that I was no longer listening to her. I felt ashamed. How unfair of me not to remember what she had been telling me for the last few minutes. I didn't know how, but I managed to tear myself away from the part of my mind preventing me from following her words and listened to what her lips were actually saying: that, although she didn't like taking her mother's advice, she understood and appreciated her point-of-view. She knew what she had to go through, with everything that had happened to her husband. "She only wants the best for us..." was the last sentence I remember her saying just before we crossed the street. We said goodbye on the other side and headed in opposite directions to our homes.

Now, she attracts me just as much or even more than she did then. But she made her choice and I ... have lost! It's like in the movies: the good-looking bloke always gets the girl, and that was that.

"Come on! Come on! Don't dawdle." Sofia's voice breaks through my inner thoughts as she grabs my right arm and leads me into the inner patio of the museum.

That's it. I mustn't dwell on it. It's time to get down to work.

We've been inside the museum for at least five minutes. We cross the inner patio. It looks like a cloister in a monastery with its rectangular floor, six columns along its longer sides and five on each of the shorter ones. I always count them when I'm here, I don't know why. I look up at the top of the columns and they look like Doric capitals, or is it Ionic? It's clear that they aren't the same as the ones at the entrance. The truth is that I can never remember. They explained it all to us at school a couple of years ago, but I have to admit that I still don't know how to tell them apart. They support the ceiling over the aisle, protecting the works on display from direct sunlight and from any rain that might enter from the central section of the open patio. In reality, the columns support an upper passage which you can just about make out from the small, long and narrow windows above, surrounding the entire patio. I've always noticed how they end in a half arch and are decorated at each end by other small columns with their curves superimposed like two Coca Cola bottles, one on top of the other.

But what I like looking at most is the decoration around the whole perimeter above those windows. It is made of dark wood and engraved with such a high degree of detail that I've always assumed that they must have been done before they were assembled. Moving around, I can feel the intense cold as I cross the patio. I look up at the sky. I can almost touch the thousands of leaves blown in and out by the persistent wind.

Looking at each side of the rectangle, on the porch side, you can see some of the sculptures or engraved stones which are part of the exhibition. I don't see anything from the period we're looking for. Directly ahead of me, Sofia is making for the far end, to the left where great black curtains reveal the entrance to the inner part of the museum they told us about. I follow her. I turn around and see that the others are also close behind. Inwardly, I smile at Sofia's ability to get others to do what she wants.

My problem is that I can't be objective where she's concerned. Everything she does is perfect.

As always when I enter this part of the museum, I have to wait a few seconds to get used to the light. In the street, although it's cold, the sun is shining, but inside it's very dark.

The first thing we see is a set of mosaics which were found in some houses in the old town during the recent restoration works. I look at Sofia. She obviously knows that this is not what she's looking for. She quickly turns and heads to the right of the room, completely sure of herself, as if she had decided beforehand what the aim of the visit was going to be.

We gather by her side. I am surrounded by my three companions standing and looking at the display cabinets. There, on display are Roman coins found at Caesaraugusta, the name given to the city by the Romans, and here they are featured everywhere.

I realise that, without thinking, I've been following Sofia around like a little lamb. I would have stayed a little longer in the inner patio to see if some of the sculptures could be Roman. She, on the other hand, takes one glance and decides that there's nothing here. I hope that we aren't making a mistake and would have to go back afterwards.

"It looks like the teacher wasn't lying." Elsa says in a loud voice, getting all of us to peer through the glass. "According to what it says here, the city was founded following a set of special instructions. It was Caesar Augustus himself who took the decision. It was founded exactly on the day of the winter's solstice and nothing short of 14 BC."

"Did you say 14 BC?" I ask, slightly alarmed, as I rummage for one of the books I have in my bag.

When at last I get it out and find the page I was looking for, I say:

"You're not going to believe the coincidence!" I look at all of them in the eye and continue, "Caesar Augustus died in 14 BC." In silence, I re-read the page, then went on, "According to this, he was 50 years old when the city was founded."

With an almost authoritarian voice and trying to be in the right, Sofia butts in:

"You seem to be looking for coincidences where there aren't any. In fact the city was founded on 23rd December and he died on 19th August. In other words, there is no coincidence."

"I wouldn't be so sure," Erik interrupts. Impatiently, Sofia turns her back on him. She doesn't like being contradicted. However, Erik carries on: "With those dates, perhaps not, but look." He points at the writing in the display cases. "According to this, the *Decumanus* was positioned so it was in line with the sunrise on 23rd December.

In other words, Emperor Augustus founded the city around the time of the winter solstice. I couldn't remember if the teacher had said it the other day in class or if someone somewhere else had mentioned it. I didn't know why, but this information struck me as both strange and mysterious at the same time. Why did he choose that exact day?

We all read the rest of the text, then go back to where we saw a map of the ancient city. Hanging on the wall, it must be around two metres wide by three metres long. I like it because it's large enough for at least a group of people like us, standing in front of it, to be able to look at it without any difficulty. What is more, it highlights the various discoveries made in the old town with tiny lights. I can easily make out the two main roads which the Romans drew to start the design.

Sofia looks back at us and puts her finger to her lips. Just then, a group of tourists approach, attentively listening to the explanation of their guide. We understand what Sofia is saying. Unnoticed, we merge with the group, although we haven't paid for the guided tour.

The guide is a tall woman, with long grey hair worn down her back. She looks around 60 years old and is wearing a long white tunic as if she were in ancient Rome. She points out the city plan to the group and explains in a loud voice the *Cardus* and the *Decumanus*, running from north to south and east to west respectively, typical of all cities built by Rome in that era.

She talks about the discoveries in the city on the map: the forum, the thermal springs, the amphitheatre and the walls. She gives a few details in response to some questions. In short, it's an ordinary explanation in an ordinary museum on an ordinary day. I'm looking at Sofia and notice that she's looking at the map in a different way. Each time the guide highlights a street, Sofia glances up at the plan again.

It seems that this isn't going to be an ordinary day after all.

I can see that she's restless. It looks as if she wants to ask something, but doesn't. This is strange because nothing usually stops her when she wants to ask something in class or in a group.

The guide goes on explaining the history of how the city was founded.

"... following this founding principle, a priest guided two oxen pulling a golden plough. He would plunge it into the earth to draw the city limits. However, in this particular case..."

Why did she say 'in this particular case'? I imagine that the Romans did it in every city. Could she have made a mistake? She must have said the same thing so many times that it was normal, totally understandable for her to make a mistake now and again. Or was it? Oh great, I thought to myself, with all this talk of a sacred city, I was starting to see nothing but mysteries wherever I looked.

"... all the earth from the furrow was piled on the inner part where the city would be built, because they understood that this was the earth of the sacred city." The guide ends her explanation and stands back a little to allow the tourists to get closer to the map.

In essence, it's the same thing they explained to us in class, but this woman seems to have lived it. She describes it as if she had actually been there. And for a moment I picture her there with her dark eyes and the furrowed skin of her face showing how the sun could leave its mark on someone. She clearly didn't get that bronze colour working in a museum. I imagine her as a busy heroine, working outdoors day after day in ancient times. Now, she's a guide in a museum. What would her life have been like then? Here I am at it again - daydreaming. I love imagining that, behind each person, there was a hidden world that only *I* have the chance to know. She would be the perfect model for my list of mysterious characters when I became a writer.

Well, that's for another time.

The guide steps forward once, pointing to the plan of the city centre, indicating that the boundary of the old town mapped out by the plough corresponded to the existing streets: Caesar Augustus and Coso. She explains that the places where the plough was lifted – four times at different points, north, south, east and west – gates would be built. Then, she says:

"One of them was called Cinegia Gate and I imagine that you have heard that name if you have passed through the city centre. Another is the Eastern Gate which later became Valencia Gate where the Church of La Magdalena is now located. To the north, there was another gate which overlooked the bridge over the Ebro River, and to the west, the gate which would later be known as the Toledo Gate, which ends at the present-day Central Market."

52

When she finishes her explanation, she moves to the next exhibition room with the group. We carry on looking at the map, or rather, hang around Sofia as she continues looking at the map.

I turn to see where the group had gone. I see that the guide is going towards another area. Then, she suddenly turns around and see that the group of young people looking at the map are missing: us. Without really meaning to, we succeeded in making her think we are part of the group and now she is coming over. She is going to tell us off and perhaps even throw us out of the museum. How embarrassing!

When the guide reaches us, Sofia steps forward, looks at her and says:

"There's something that I don't understand." She stops and looks directly at the guide. "Up to now, we've always seen this map of the city centre with the *Cardus* and the *Decumanus* intersecting. In class, they told us that Zaragoza was chosen by the Romans for the intersection created by the Gallego and Huerva Rivers as they flowed into the Ebro. The rivers correspond to this north-south and east-west orientation, but if we put this city plan that you have shown us and we orient it correctly, Don Jaime Street and the Calle Mayor..."

Sofia stops and then, looking directly at her, says:

"...do not run either north-south, or east-west."

There's silence.

All eyes are fixed on the guide, expecting a snappy response. Sofia never ceases to amaze me. I don't understand why she asked the question, but I thought the answer would be forthcoming in a matter of seconds.

But it isn't. We watch in astonishment as the guide turns red but says nothing. She shakes her head from side to side, stopping as soon as she sees that the guard, standing at the entrance of the room, is looking at her. She presses her lips together as if trying to seal her mouth. She looks so nervous.

To break the ice, I say to Sofia in low voice:

"She doesn't know the answer."

Sofia gives me a disapproving look. Then, she turns back to the guide. We are all waiting for her answer. She then surprises us again because, without saying a word, she turns on her heels and walks back to her group. The four of us look at each other with puzzled expressions, not knowing what just happened. Without much ado, we continue our visit through the museum to finish our class assignment.

The rest of the exhibition isn't as interesting. We keep on walking briskly through the aisles.

At last, our visit comes to an end. Sofia stays a bit behind us in the inner patio, looking at a monolith apparently from the Roman era. The rest of us stand at the door, waiting for her. Just when we're about to leave the museum, we all look back at Sofia in the distance. She must have realised that we're looking at her and looks as if she didn't understand what we were saying, making the usual hand signals. She finally turns her back to us, I notice her alarm as she sees the guide silently approaching her. She's looking straight at Sofia, holding out her hand as if bidding her farewell.

Sofia looks surprised by this gesture normally reserved for adults. She responds by offering her own. They shake hands. The guide murmurs something, which we couldn't hear.

Then, the woman in her white tunic disappears into the interior. Our friend stands transfixed, leaning against one of the columns.

She doesn't speak, but simply stares at her fist, which, even from a distance, we can make out is clenched around a small piece of white paper, jutting out from the side of her hand.

CHAPTER 7

Thursday 15 December 2016
Time: 11:00 am

Sofia

Going into a museum is normally really boring, especially if you don't have a clear mission. It was my dad who made my brother, sister, and me look for something more in such places. Not that we had not travelled a lot in our lives. In the past two years during the summer holidays, we had been to England, France and Italy in the same summer, at my dad's insistence. The truth was that it wasn't so dictatorial of him, because when he first brought it up, we all thought it was a very good idea. Three different countries in the same summer, great! That was my initial thought when he said it.

The five of us had always made decisions on where to go together on holiday, until this last summer. A day in May, we would agree on a time when each member in the family could propose where to go and what to do. I had always thought that my parents were a little strange. When I asked my friends who else did this, I realised that they were unique. In none of my friends' families did they do something similar. I liked the idea because each of us could make a suggestion and we all ended up laughing. It was very good, especially because I realised in later years that they did it so that we would learn geography. We had to give a presentation to the others, using maps showing where we wanted to go. Initially, in earlier years, we used an atlas, but later on we had to design the holiday in front of a computer screen, using the internet to look at, move and enlarge maps as much as we wanted.

So, two years ago, when he suggested it, his proposal was successful and we had a very good time. The strange thing was that, the following year, he suggested the same thing. However, this time, he proposed that we visited the three cities where we had spent the most time the previous year: London, Paris and Bergamo. He put it to us in such a way that night, that my brother, sister, my mother and I all looked at one other in surprise. We weren't able to come up with another suggestion.

So we returned and had a great time once again.

However, there was something that was different from before. I remember that, in the following year, my dad disappeared for a whole day in each of the three cities and he never told us what he had done on his *free Father's Day*, as he called it to justify it. My mother didn't seem to mind because it was clear that she knew what he was doing. They really got on very well, although they were very different people. One was like the mountain and the other like the valley, but that was the most special thing about them because they always came to an agreement.

The problem is that last summer was the last time we went on holiday together.

What I remember most of the visits to those three cities were the museums he took us to. We went to the most important ones and, in each, he invented a kind of treasure hunt. I will never forget when, in the middle of the National Art Gallery in London, as she entered the room, my sister shouted out, "a Van Gogh!" Everyone in the room turned around to look at her. We felt embarrassed, but our parents were full of pride.

They made everything special. When we visited Paris, we had to draw the facade of the Notre-Dame Cathedral and count how many statues and geometrical shapes there were. And we did it, although I have to admit that it was a condition they gave us for going to Disneyland the following day. We of course completed the task without complaining.

But I never got to go with him to the Zaragoza Municipal Museum, which is also called the Provincial Museum. The most important and the oldest one in the city, we had never visited it together. I wonder what kind treasure hunt he would have organised for us there. I would never know.

At least, he taught us to enjoy looking for things which others might overlook. When we visited a museum, he would typically ask: "How many people do you think would have noticed that?" So today, I pause for a long time to look at a large stone in the museum.

As the sign said, it was a piece of an ashlar from the Eastern Gate of the Roman city, which they later called Valencia Gate. The explanation is on a small white card next to the stone. It's a quadrangular piece of masonry, worked in grey limestone, 80 cm wide by 57 cm tall and 91 cm thick. On the left side of the face there are some inscriptions in six lines of Roman lettering. I try to read them, but not all the lines are complete. On the right side, there's no inscription, but it's obvious that there was once something there because it's been worn away as if by some kind of tool that erased what was written, making it illegible.

Suddenly, all that slips from my mind when the guide comes up and speaks to me. I don't know what surprises me more, her words or, when I shake her hand, I notice a crumpled piece of paper she leaves in my palm after we release our hands as she says goodbye with a conspiratorial smile.

For a moment, I remain frozen, incapable of moving. Then, I turn around. I remain standing alone next to the stone I was studying. The guide has disappeared and my friends are looking at me from a few metres away. For a moment, I thought she was mad. However, the way she looked at me and spoken to me was completely sane, but she had a certain air of mystery about her.

Looking at the people around me at the time, I see that the museum guard has noticed what happened. I don't think he's seen the paper, but he's calling someone on his mobile. He's looking at the guide. Our eyes met and, without taking his eyes off me, he speaks very briefly on the phone. Whatever was said to him must have made him uneasy because he quickly looks away and disappears once more through the black curtains to the room with the mural of the city with the *Cardus* and *Decumanus*.

I continue standing in the patio next to the monolith. My friends have not budged from where they are standing and are still looking at me.

I open the paper and read its contents. Below some text, there's a drawing of a circle and within it a rectangle in which there are lines linking two halves of the rectangle. A small shape, made up of two squares, is located where the inner lines meet. What strikes me most is that, in contrast to the sides of the paper and the text above it, the rectangle is tilted a little to the right.

I don't know what to make of it. My friends continue to look on. Just then, there's a commotion as two groups of tourists come together, one finishing their guided tour and the other about to start. We find ourselves among a crowd of people and I'm totally amazed to see Elsa who, with great skill and effort, makes a perfect path between the two groups for us to leave the museum.

She's incredible. The next time I find myself trapped in a crowd of people, I would want Elsa at my side.

"Thanks a lot," I say, with a wink, when I catch up with her.

It probably helps that she's so big and tall (in fact, she's as tall as Erik and a key player in her basketball team), with her dark complexion contrasting greatly with that of the other people there. Moreover, she's wearing a long black coat and a white woollen cap with a visor covering her hair. Having put up her collar, she has a certain air of importance. When she stretches her arms out between the people there for them to make way with a big smile on her face, everyone moves aside and regards her seriously. By the expression on their faces, they think that she's part of the museum staff.

Suddenly, the guard, who was inside earlier, comes up behind her, seizes her hand and whispers something in her ear. With a grimace of pain, Elsa pulls away hard from him to escape his grasp. She makes a gesture as if she doesn't understand, which isn't surprising, given all the racket that's taking place. The man is now speaking louder, and so I go closer to hear him.

"Take your friend away from here immediately and take no notice of anything she tells you!"

Swinging her arms amid the shouts and shoves from other people, Elsa manages to free herself from the man. She looks at him, frowning with hostility as he slips away, disappearing from sight. She looks at me, wide-eyed, lowering her arms and allowing the crowd to carry her along towards the exit. We look at each other and shrug our shoulders.

The crowd drags us along until we find ourselves together at the entrance.

"What shit is this?" Elsa asks me, straining every muscle on her face. "Who's that guy?"

"I have no idea," I reply.

From her expression, I can see that she's as confused as I am.

With everyone's nervousness, what happened with the guide and afterwards the incident with the guard left me quite confused and so distracted that, as I leave the museum, I stumble over two well-dressed people who have collapsed in the street. I almost scream out of fear, but I manage to control myself. This is madness! What's happening to this city? I turn to the guard at the door, pointing at the people on the ground. He merely shrugs his shoulders, shortly before raising his hand to his ear and closing his eyes as if something was suddenly irritating him. The moment quickly passes, although I can see a drop of blood trickling down from his left ear. He stops looking at me and, in the confusion, tries to help the two groups entering and leaving at the same time. Unable to do so, he finally sits down on the chair behind him.

If I am surprised, it's nothing compared to Elsa and David. Erik is less expressive, but I think that, deep down, he's as disconcerted as we are. We look all around us. On every corner of the plaza, there's someone on the ground.

"What's happening here? Everyone's collapsing in the street," David remarks.

"What shocks me more," Elsa responds, "is that passers-by don't seem at all surprised by all the people who have collapsed."

"No adult seems bothered. So, we shouldn't let it bother us either," I say as we leave the museum. "Let's finish the work we have to present before Christmas."

At that moment, everyone turns towards me and stares at me in silence. I take out the paper that the guide at the museum gave me. They look at the crumpled paper on which, as I smooth it out, they can see what's printed on it: *Calle Mayor 1, 8th Floor*, and the symbol.

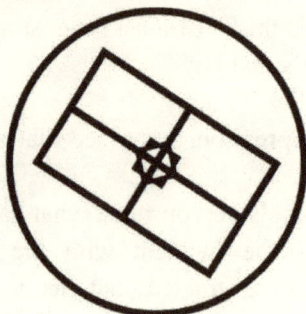

They all look at me and David asks:

"Apart from giving you the note, did she say anything?"

I remain pensive for a moment, and after a moment's silence, I repeat the precise words the guide said to me: "Visit him. He will give you the answer," I quote word for word.

CHAPTER 8

Thursday 15 December 2016
Time: 3:30 pm

David

If it had not been for rowing training set for today, I would have stayed longer. I would have liked to have been alone with Sofia. She would have told me, *only* me, what exactly the guide at the museum had told her. I would have liked to sit with her alone on a bench in the plaza opposite the museum. As I put my arm around her shoulders, she would have rested her redhead on my chest. She would have told me, only me, what she was feeling. I'm sure that she was not afraid, but she must have felt something when the woman gave her that paper. I want to know.

When she had told me everything, I would have stroked her hair. Then, unexpectedly, she would have looked up directly into my eyes. We would have sat like this for a couple of seconds until she lowered her gaze to my lips. Unexpectedly, she would put her left hand behind my neck...

"Hey, David. What's up? Where are you, man?"

Jon's words break through my reverie. I'm daydreaming again. I can't believe it. The problem is that, lately, it's happening to me all too often... and it's about her.

"Nothing, it's nothing," I lie. "Pass me some water please."

As I point at the bottle on the table, I glance at the other ten members of the rowing team. They have already served the second course. I must have drifted away from the conversation, caught up in my own thoughts.

At least I've remained with the dream because, just as Sofia was showing us the paper the guide had given her at the exit of the museum, I had to leave quickly as the rowing team was having their Christmas meal.

The team is like my second family. We get on very well together. We've been training together for almost six years and it's not been too bad. Didn't we win the first prize in the national competition four or five times? I can never remember exactly how many times because I often confuse them with the regional competitions we've won. Well, it doesn't matter. Anyone looking at us from a distance would say that we were all cut from the same cloth: same height, same complexion. I think that the only thing that distinguishes us is our hair colour because even the depth of our tan is the same on account of the number of hours we train together.

"Here," Jon comes across with the bottle and, smiling ironically, he serves me a glass.

"What's the matter?" I ask him, in response to this half-challenging gaze.

Jon and I became friends the very same day he arrived at our school, four years ago. He came from Bilbao and his family had decided to settle in this city because of the reputation of the rowing team. Even though the Ebro River does not look too clean, it's maintained a very good water level and traditionally, this sport has always been practised here. During training, I can completely escape from reality. I end up continuously needing to have this feeling. However, for the next few days during the Christmas holidays, we aren't going to train. I think it's going to be hard for me.

"It's about a girl, isn't it?"

I return his look. In the same week, both my mother and my best friend have said the same thing. We're so close that it's difficult to keep secrets from each other.

But I don't want to share this.

"No, no," I lie again. "It's my mother. She looks sadder every day, more distant."

At that moment, Coach stands up. He's around 30. Having lost most of his hair, he decided to shave his head completely bald the year before. With massively broad shoulders and super muscular arms, he looks like a character from one of those

American movies about prisoners, who are locked away and occasionally get involved in fights. Today, he's happy – a rare occurrence because, in training, he's the hardest man I know. What's good about him is that when he's relaxed, he's a completely different person and will even tell jokes. Now, he's lifting his glass of water and shouts:

"Merry Christmas, everyone!"

We all do the same and shout back so loudly that it makes the 20 people, who together with us have filled the little restaurant in the Old Town, turn around.

"MERRY CHRISTMAS, COACH!"

Suddenly, the same unpleasant feeling I've had all week is happening again. This time, it's even more shocking because of the loud crash of shattering glass.

The glass the coach has been holding is now smashed and scattered all over the floor. Everyone around is splashed with water. And he... he's falling. He quickly grabs hold of the table to support himself. Those around him try to grab hold of his muscular mass, but to no avail.

Dear God, he's bleeding from his left ear!

He puts up his hand to stop the bleeding. Then he loses his balance and we hear his head hitting the table. Everyone in the restaurant turns around to see what's happening. As the adults watch on, they remain sitting. My companions sitting close to the coach rush towards him. Some have taken out their mobile phones and are frantically calling the ambulance. The noise is enormous as it resounds through the restaurant. I notice that some people have begun to run out of the room. All I can hear was noise and more noise. I feel powerless to act.

Wide-eyed, Jon looks at me. He's pale.

"What's happening?"

I stare at him. I can't look away. I can almost see every detail of the pupils in his eyes.

I can't respond. I'm thinking only of all that's occurred in previous days.

CHAPTER 9

Thursday 15 December 2016
Time: 4:30 pm

Sofia

"Okay Mum, I'm leaving now."

"So soon, dear?" she asks me as I stand up from the table.

Today, she looks prettier. For the past few days, she has looked worried, as if expecting something to happen. She can't stop pacing around the house. She goes in and out of my father's office which has remained untouched since he left. The times when I walk along the corridor and see her inside, I stop to observe her. She walks around the room, looking at everything. She lifts his papers from his desk and then puts them back down again. She picks up the briefcase that he has on the floor. She opens it, looks inside, closes it again and then returns it to the floor, against the wall. It's fast becoming a routine. Since my father's disappearance, she's been doing it again and again. But in recent days, she has done it more often. Furthermore, she keeps calling her sister. And one day, she's even laughed on the phone, something she has seldom done in the last year.

I watch her as she sits at the kitchen table with my brother and sister who are observing all that she is doing. My little sister can't help giggling each time our mum gets up and moves around the kitchen. With her right elbow on the table, she never takes her eyes off my mother.

I go up to my mother and without saying anything, I give her a hug as she's sitting there. I notice how she rests her face against me and allows me to stroke it. How proud I am of her!

The doorbell rings.

"That's Erik!" I say quickly as I make my way towards the door. "We're working very hard on the History project. The group that I have is very nice," I say, to excuse my haste.

"Who's in your group?" I feel that she's asking because she doesn't want to miss the slightest detail of what's happening in my life. I like that.

"There's David..." I begin to count on my fingers as if we're a large group. "The one who was in my class since I was small." My mother smiles, but I don't understand why. "Then, Elsa, Samuel, the strange boy, and Erik. It's all going very well..."

My mom looks at me because I stop and cannot continue. Wide-eyed and with her arms on the table, she stands up. She approaches me, puts her hands on my shoulders and asks:

"Is everything alright, dear?"

My mother's words would have obliged me to tell her everything that had happened to us, from what had happened to the teacher in class, the guide at the museum, the paper and the people who were losing their balance on the street. But, I don't know if what's on my mind is nonsense or not. I prefer to confirm it first before saying anything to her.

"Yes, yes of course, mum," I answer, surprised by the banality of my response. "I've to go now as we've agreed to meet up on Alfonso Street."

I kiss her and wave goodbye to my sister and brother. They say goodbye, and I rush off.

I normally use the stairs to go down the seven floors, but today it is quicker to use the lift. Four, three, two... I like looking at the numbers on the indicator. Zero, at last. I push open the door to open for Erik but he's already inside the entrance. In fact, I opened it for him with the automatic door opener when I told him on the intercom that I was coming down.

No sooner do I close the door to the lift when he approaches me. He looks at me, puts his arms around me and I feel his hands on the lower part of my back. I tiptoe and look into his eyes. There's no one in the entrance lobby, nor can anyone see us from the street because Erik already knows where the blind spot is around the exit from the lifts. Hence, we do what only the two of us know about.

Suddenly, we are startled. On pure reflex, we pull apart.

A resident has called the lift to the second floor and the noise abruptly brings the moment to an end. We see the lift going up. We look at each other, and like little children caught red-handed doing something naughty, we smile at each other.

Erik takes me by the shoulder and we go out into the street, heading for Plaza Aragon.

"You look very pretty," he compliments me as we walk together.

I stop, remove his hand from my shoulder and move away from him. Then, I look at him and say:

"But you've hardly looked at me."

He laughs and looks me up and down. He almost makes me blush when he stops a couple of times.

"Stop looking at me like that!" I snap at him. Then, I grab his hand and pull him along to continue walking.

Just as we are about to cross at the light on Paseo Constitución, Erik stops.

"Why did you mention it to the guide at the museum?" He turns and looks at me tenderly.

He's taken me by surprise. I'm simply looking at the people crossing the street with us.

"Because..." I begin and pause, tentatively, since the man on our right appears to have stopped to listen to us. When I see him moving away, I continue: "The other day in class, when the teacher explained it, there was something that did not quite add up."

He's looking at me, searching every corner of my face. I answered the question he's asked, but he doesn't seem to be paying any attention to what I'm saying. He stops his wandering gaze and now, his eyes are fixed on my mouth.

"I like you so much, Sofia."

Before I realise what's happening, he kisses me on the mouth in the middle of the street. What is he doing? I've already told him that I don't like people seeing us kissing in public.

But I like it. I feel that tingling sensation again deep within me when he did it.

Then, he takes my hand and, seizing the initiative, he continues walking towards Paseo Independencia.

Suddenly, quite unexpectedly, he asks:

"By the way, is there anything between you and David?" He inquires, as he continues walking without even looking at me, and then adds: "He looks at you strangely."

I'm unable to answer him.

CHAPTER 10

Thursday 15 December 2016
Time: 5:00 pm

David

Since they pedestrianised Alfonso Street a few years ago, people in the city are more willing to walk through the old town. They stop at leisure in the old shopping centre. They walk down to the river and then end up at the Basilica. Whenever I look down the street from where I'm standing, I always want to go down to the end. I love buying those sweets that are so typical of Zaragoza to go chasing the pigeons through Plaza del Pilar afterwards. I'm sure that there will be many of them competing to eat the seeds the children scatter on the ground. When you see them, they're all wanting to catch a pigeon in their hands to take a photo.

I remember doing this with my father and little brother when I was little. I wouldn't even consider doing that now at my age. My father is no longer with us and at 16, I'm not going to run after those birds. What would people think if they saw me?!

It's a long wait at the top of the street, but I'm aware that I've arrived ten minutes early. Moreover, the coach's fainting spell has left me nervous. He's the second person, close to me, that I've seen suffer in recent days.

Behind me, there's Coso Street, where they've closed off traffic to build two tramways, without leaving space for vehicles and pedestrians to circulate at the same time without danger. It's better, I think. I prefer it this way, compared to what it was before.

I'm surrounded by buildings which make me feel that I'm at the end of the 19th century. As mentioned in class, after the War of Independence the city invested in the restoration of the Old Town, and Alfonso Street is the area which underwent the greatest transformation. Rich people from that period had to follow certain building standards, which has continued for the most part to this present day, allowing us to enjoy their symmetry, the same heights, with viewing points built out of iron and crystal in the chamfers of the buildings. It's a quiet journey back into the past with a single glance.

From here, the landscape never ceases to amaze me, not so much for its architectural surroundings, but for its people. The mix is incredible. Although it's winter, and despite the strong cold *cierzo* wind blowing, the street is full. People of different age groups are converging on the same road – groups, lone individuals, couples, families, different cultures and races, some stopping at shops, others just having a stroll, but all going in the same direction: towards Coso Street or the Basilica del Pilar (Basilica of Our Lady of the Pillar), with very few dipping into the little side alleyways.

What surprises me most is the perceived balance in the city, so much diversity... in harmony. This is one of the places where it's most evident. So, I've come before to see it.

"Have you been waiting long?"

I jump. I'm so lost in my thoughts that I've not heard them coming up behind me.

"Sorry." I glance at Elsa's face as she apologises. My expression must have betrayed me. "We have startled you."

I see that Sofia and Erik, holding hands, have joined her. I notice that Sofia releases Erik's hand when she sees me looking at them. The three of them have arrived at the same time.

"No, don't worry about it," I answer, turning quickly around to face the Basilica. "I was looking at the view from here."

Sofia steps forward to stand next to me to look down to the end of the street.

"I've always wondered," she starts saying as the others also turn to look down the street, "why this geometry was off-centred. It is as if the logical balance in the alignment have been distorted."

Balance! I've heard nothing else but this word lately. But, I don't know what she means by it at this moment.

"Do you see the central dome?" Sofia continues, looking fixedly at it. "It is out of place in this view and the image of the Virgin on the wall of the Basilica is not aligned with the centre of the street."

I've never seen it that way. I move towards the centre to get a better look. She's right! It looks strange and somewhat distorted. The architecture does not geometrically coincide with the position of the street. I look again. This time, something else distracts me and breaks the balance. It's the person who's walking towards us.

If the majority of people walk in either of the two directions, there will always be someone cutting across them, coming from one of the alleyways on the left. He will obviously bump into any pedestrians crossing his path.

If neither my friends nor I are wearing attention grabbing clothes, this one certainly is.

"Hi!"

That's all he says. He remains standing next to us in silence. He turns around to look down the street as we've been doing. I'm sure that we'll not get anything more out of him for the rest of the afternoon. In the end, it's what we have to put up with.

The day the tutor read out the names of the members for each team organised by the History teacher, he began reading the names of the four of us sitting in the first two rows. It certainly wasn't the best thing to happen to me that week as, ever since Sofia started going out with Erik, I've tried to hide my feelings towards her with behaviour that, at times, bordered on being rude, and she's noticed it. But when the tutor read out Samuel's name as part of our group, I had a start. I saw shock registered all over Elsa's face, sitting next to me. I couldn't see Sofia's face, only her back. But from Erik's expression as he turned to look at Sofia, I saw that my Swedish friend was also surprised by it. I'm sure that they didn't have anyone quite so weird in his school back in his country.

To describe it in another way, Samuel is different from the rest of the class. He dresses only in black T-shirts. He always wears his hair long and dishevelled. He's short and never seems to take care of himself. For most of the year, but less frequently in summer, he wears a black coat that reaches down to his knees. It makes him look fat because his pockets are stuffed with things. What stands out from his dark and somewhat slovenly clothes are his shoes: he wears absolutely white trainers. This year, I notice that they are always spotless and always the same brand.

He has no friends at school. As classes finish, he goes home. Nobody knows where he lives. No one has seen his parents at school. However, Samuel has two noteworthy qualities: he gets the best marks in class and he has the strongest local accent I've ever heard. He's a guy of few words, but when he speaks, he makes you feel a certain sympathy for him. The problem is that I think that he's not shaved since he began to grow a beard two years before. His unwashed and untidy appearance generates a certain amount of repudiation. Moreover, if you try to strike up a conversation with him, you won't get many words strung together in a sentence.

So, it isn't pleasant having him in our team as he doesn't like working in a group. I therefore feel that the rest of us will end up having to do all the work ourselves. If at least he said something...

"Hi," Sofia greets him. "How are you? Have you analysed all that I told you about what had happened in the museum? I am sure that you have written everything in detail."

"Yes." He answers briefly, at no point looking at her directly.

It's true. This is our second visit to the city after they set us this work. He couldn't come the first time because, according to him, he was in bed with fever. Sofia told us that she had called him afterwards to tell him what had happened to us. What a story to tell on the phone!

I observe how she looks it at him. I can't work out if it is with gentleness or collusion. However, ever since I've known her, since the time we were little, she has always been the one who treated everyone very well. I realise that they are the first words that they exchanged in public since we started this project.

As he doesn't say anything more, I break silence:

"Shall we start on what we have planned for today?" I then begin to walk down the street towards the Basilica.

We've only just started walking when Erik points at an ice cream shop in the first block, in the building on our left. As it's not the first time that this Nordic boy has insisted on the goodness of eating ice cream in the middle of winter, on this occasion I choose not to argue and follow him. The others do likewise, even Samuel on my left hurries ahead of Erik and reaches the door first. We all have a small bag or backpack with us. He, on the other hand, is not carrying anything, except his coat and, I guess, everything he has stuffed into his pockets.

As we reach the glass door, it opens automatically. We look inside. It's all painted in white. The few pink decorations make it look as if you are at the North Pole... for girls, because everything is pink. However, I like this ice cream shop, where they sell yoghourt ice cream. You choose the flavour you want and then on the ice cream base, they add the other ingredients to 'dress' it as you want.

The shop assistant must have been two or three years older than us. She's of average height, slim, with black hair in a low ponytail. By the uncertain way she serves us, it appears that she's only been working there for a few days. However, with those green eyes and that beautiful smile, I'm sure that she will get on fast and soon. I see her attending to a group of four girls who are around my age. In spite of the cold, they have on short miniskirts, but from the clothes they're wearing, it was obvious that colour combination isn't their strong point.

The atmosphere turns bizarre because the other group of people in the shop are a couple with two small children. The baby has been crying from the moment we entered and the mother tries in vain to soothe him. The father is shouting at the older girl who must have been no more than four years old.

I couldn't understand why he's scolding her, but he's creating a very tense atmosphere in the ice cream parlour. The more he shouts, the more the baby cries. The mother is growing nervous and it's becoming harder to calm the infant. They must have been there a long time, trying to eat ice cream, as they sit on the armchairs located on the right in the little shop.

I notice that the little girl has soiled her clothes with the ice cream. From their appearance, I can describe them as being different. The man is quite a good few years older than the woman. They all have dark hair. The only contrast is the pale white skin of the baby, compared to the very dark complexion of the child and her parents. My friends are probably drawing their own conclusions.

We look at each other, observing the scene without knowing what to say. I see the shop assistant glancing nervously at them. The girls in the miniskirts keep arguing among themselves about the suitability of a different ingredient or other on the yoghourt ice cream they have chosen. It seems to be the most important decision they have to make all day. They're making me nervous. One is as good as the other if in the end you are going to eat it, I would tell them.

"Please, could you lower your voice?" the young assistant dares to ask the man who's shouting.

She's not as uncertain as she appears.

The impact is enormous. As the girl speaks to the man, there's absolute silence. Even the baby is quiet. The assistant's South American accent resounds through the shop. We all remain even quieter, waiting to see what's going to happen afterwards. The girls ordering their ice creams are startled. One of them holding the first ice cream ends up without it as she drops it on the ground. The angry man stands up and glares in fury at the assistant. Instinctively, she steps back behind the counter.

"How dare you!" He shouts as he strides towards her. "Who do you think you are?" He shouts even louder.

Sofia and Elsa become alarmed. I glance at Erik. Without saying a word, we take advantage of our height as we are more than a foot taller than him. In a single step, the two of us stand in front of him, putting up a barrier between this savage and the counter.

"But, what's this?" He bellows again, looking up at us.

I can feel the force of his fury in his step and clenched fists. Erik and I flex our muscles and fold our arms in front of us. The girls in the miniskirts look at us and giggle among themselves. Sofia is soothing the little girl who, still frightened and crying, runs to the person closest to her.

"What a shitty ice cream parlour!" He shouts, as he grabs the little girl's hand. With one tug, he yanks the child away from Sofia and strides towards the exit. "I will never come back here again!" He yells again, now close to the street.

At that moment, something that none of us had anticipated happens.

The matter would have been settled perfectly well if the man had simply left. But, the door does not open. As he propels himself forward, expecting the motion detector to open the two glass doors towards the sides, he collides against the door. He loses his balance and falls to the ground.

The incident in the ice cream shop is like a scene from a horror film. The young girls move closer to the wall for protection. They huddle tightly among themselves. The shop assistant stands petrified behind the counter. The baby begins to scream even more loudly. The little girl escapes from her father and runs back to Sofia, hiding her face in my friend's coat. Elsa goes to the mother and gives the baby a small toy she has in her backpack to get him to be quiet. Erik and I make a gesture to help the man to his feet, but he rudely rejects our offer.

74

I have never heard such loud shouting coming out of a man's mouth. I can't distinguish between the children's screams and the man's yelling. He continues hurling abuse at the shop assistant with every humiliating and racist expletive he can think of.

"That's enough!" I shout, standing in front of him. "You don't have the right to mistreat anyone in this way! It is not her fault!"

"You have to calm down!" Erik joined me, shouting at the man.

The man continues shouting. He again heads for the door for it to open. But it doesn't. He repeats the movement several times with the same result. Elsa leaves the mother and, very coolly, approaches the shop assistant. I hear her gentle words asking her to activate the mechanism to open the door. However, the shop assistant is frozen to the spot and begins to cry.

I don't know where to turn - the group of frightened girls sobbing in the corner, the baby crying inconsolably at his mother's breast or the little dark-haired girl in Sofia's arms sobbing with her face hidden in her coat. The man has become even more agitated and begins breaking some of the few pieces of furniture in the shop. Erik and I look at each other with blank expressions. We too are frozen into inaction, not knowing what to do: whether to block the man, keep the people apart or call the police on the mobile.

But there's someone else in the shop.

It's some time before I begin to look around. I turn around in all directions trying to locate Samuel. What happens next makes my blood curdle. Samuel must have gone to the back of the shop. Suddenly, he strides towards the entrance. He grabs the chair from the man just as the man is about to break it against the wall near where the girls are cowering. Without a word, Samuel sets the chair next to him. Shocked by what has just happened, the man is stunned.

Except for the baby, everyone falls silent. We all watch as Samuel takes out a screwdriver from an inner pocket in his coat. Then, he mounts the chair. He raises himself up in order not to lose his balance. With a skill that I would never have imagined this freak had, he opens the connection box controlling the sliding door and operates the mechanism.

In less than a minute the doors open again. With great satisfaction, we feel the icy wind entering from the street.

Samuel continues working on the device. He moves his left hand towards the detector. We watch the little light alternating from green to red, each time he makes the door open by his movement and waits some seconds until it closes again. When he is satisfied, he closes the box casing with his screwdriver, gets down from the chair, leaves it where it was and returns the screwdriver to his coat pocket. Then, he quietly stands in front of the man, and stares at him. They are the same height. The silence is intense. Even the baby is quiet. If it were possible, he might have recorded the whole scene in his little head.

For as long as I live, I don't think that I will ever be able to understand the look that Samuel gave that man. What I will remember is how this raging lunatic suddenly calms down. He takes his little daughter's hand, helps his wife carefully to stand up with the baby and leaves the ice cream shop in silence. This time, the glass doors open to allow the family to leave.

We all look at Samuel. I believe that I speak not only for myself. I believe that this is the beginning of a new relationship with this guy. I've just discovered something that I was not expecting, and I really like it. In fact, I am proud that he's part of our group.

Then, suddenly, to everyone's surprise, he goes up to the counter and, in his strong Zaragoza accent, he asks the assistant:

"Could I please have a tub of yoghourt ice cream with a topping of caramel and caramelised nuts?"

I don't know who's more surprised, the waitress or the rest of us looking on.

Just at that moment, Sofia grasps our arms and draws us to where she is:

"Did you see the pendant the little girl was wearing?" she asks, looking intently at each of us.

We are speechless.

"Yes," Samuel breaks the silence. "It's the same symbol they gave you in the museum."

We all turn to look at Samuel. He's full of surprises, especially when he's not yet seen it. The description that Sofia had given him was enough.

"When did you realise?" asked Sofia.

"As soon as we entered the shop."

How observant! I've always considered myself very observant, but I hadn't even noticed it. Nor did the others, judging from their expressions. Sofia must have seen it when the child was sobbing against her.

"Now there's no time to waste," Sofia says nervously. "We have to follow them to find out how the little girl got the symbol."

We all stare at her. Only Samuel breaks the silence.

"Sorry, I am having my ice cream," he said as he approaches the counter, looking at the shop assistant.

"Me too." Elsa, Erik and I respond eagerly, all at the same time, exchanging conspiratorial looks between us and smiling in collusion.

CHAPTER 11

Thursday 15 December 2016
Time: 6:30 pm

Sofia

"It was good, wasn't it?"

Erik's voice whispers in my ear, bringing me back to reality.

I'm lost in my thoughts again, thinking about what happened in the ice cream shop. I don't know what surprised me most – the behaviour of the hysterical man, the frightened assistant, the silly hysterical girls, David and Erik standing up to the man, Samuel dealing with the problem, or the child with the pendant. I can't stop thinking about that symbol. If only I knew what it meant, and why the child was wearing it.

And the mother, how she looked at me when I touched the pendant to look at it more closely! Was it curiosity or fear I saw etched on her face? I have not yet told the others about that.

And here he is asking me about the ice cream.

"I don't know," I reply looking at the people around as the five of us make our way down Alfonso Street towards the Basilica del Pilar. "I don't want any ice cream. I want to talk to the mother to ask her where she got the child's pendant from."

He does not realise that I've noticed his shrug of indifference. Shadows often give us away.

"I would like to know myself." David said, to support me.

At least someone else in the group isn't thinking only of ice cream in this commotion. Suddenly, Erik grabs me and pulls me towards him.

"Careful!" he shouts.

I don't try to pull away. Samuel, walking on my left, jumps to the opposite side, allowing the corpulent man walking in front of us to fall backwards. The woman with him is shouting. The crash is very loud because he's fallen straight down like a tree trunk and has hit his head. Dear me, there's blood on the ground! A trickle is coming out of his ear, but even worse, it's forming a small pool of blood under his head.

"Move away! Quickly!"

A couple of policemen on patrol push us aside to make room to attend to the man. People start gathering around. The woman has stopped screaming and is now crying while being comforted by two women who've been walking along the street. As people push forward to see what is happening, we are forced to move away and withdraw to the wall of the cafe on the left.

Samuel takes out his tablet from one of his pockets and starts taking photos of the people. The rest of us, like petrified bodies, are leaning against the glass frontage of the café as we look on. No one says anything.

Suddenly, there's shouting and pounding on the glass. Erik releases me and points behind us. David turns around to look and, with disgust, walks up the street towards the corner where the bank is. Elsa turns and shows her annoyance. It's incredible! People in the café start insulting and shouting at us from inside to move away and not block their view of the spectacle happening in the street. Such elegant, well-dressed couples are shouting at us. How disgusting!

We all move away, not before Elsa start making a couple of rude signs with her finger, which could have caused us problems if someone had come out.

As we reach the corner of Torre Nueva Street, to get away from all this confusion, I make signs for us to turn around and continue walking towards Plaza San Felipe.

"Look!" David shouts, looking back towards Alfonso Street.

Samuel turns around, takes his tablet out again to take photos and walks back two steps. The rest of us only turn around. What we see leaves us dumbstruck.

There are three people on the ground holding their ears. We are some 20 metres away, but I can see that the hands of the three people are covered in blood and that they are just staring at it. They try to stand, but collapse again. They can't stay on their feet.

Suddenly, one of the policemen who went to the aid of the corpulent man is falling backwards in a daze. He has his hands up against his ears. Then, his legs buckle under him. Fortunately, he manages to put his left hand down on the ground to break his fall. Otherwise, he would have collapsed like the man who had fallen earlier.

"We can't do anything here." Samuel surprises us in his matter-of-fact tone, as he puts his tablet away again into his pocket, turns and walks in the direction of Plaza San Felipe.

"Why not?" Elsa asks. "We could call the police."

Then, she falls quiet. As if speaking for the others, I point towards Alfonso Street and say:

"But if the police are there..."

I walk towards Samuel and then head towards the Plaza.

"Come, I want to see something," I declare.

Everything is beginning to get intense - the guide at the museum, the conflict in the ice cream shop, the commotion on the street just now. I need a little peace and quiet, and the place we are going towards has always been a haven of peace for me...

There are several people walking in the opposite direction to where we are going. I think that they have probably heard about what's happening behind us. I glance at my friends. They seem very serious with expressionless faces, as if waiting for something else to happen. We're some metres away from the corner of Plaza San Felipe. Walking along the street and occupying its whole width, we look like a band of cowboys from those American Westerns entering a street to confront the crooks. Samuel's broad coat, which he wears unbuttoned, and Elsa's, although a little narrow, also unfastened, helps to conjure up the image of the five of us coming in from the Wild West.

Caught up in our thoughts, we at last reach my haven of peace. I like this plaza. The Casa Montal restaurant on the right, with its old but well-kept building, invites you to travel back in time. Opposite in the background, stand the Pablo Gargallo Museum and the Church of San Felipe on the left. Whenever I look at it, I'm constantly looking for a second tower to give symmetry to the entrance. Of course I can never find it. Neither do I ever stop admiring the door at the entrance into the church which, according to my mother, was originally the door to the Basilica del Pilar in the city, but was brought here to this church.

I again look at the two statues at the entrance of the museum. Each has a rider mounted on a horse which, on many a Sunday morning, has a bottle or a piece of clothing forgotten by some absent-minded person from a party the night before. That sometimes occurs to works of art.

I head for the place I want to go to. Behind, the others stop to look at me.

I reach the statue of the little boy sitting on the ground and looking up, with his legs bent at the knees and his arms resting on them, and I sit down next to it.

"Is this why you wanted us to come here?" Erik asks as he reaches me.

The others laugh. David and Elsa also sit down next to me.

"I love this place," I say, looking at the place where the statue is. "I don't know why they put it here, but I like coming here. It's so peaceful here."

"You really don't know why they put it there?"

Elsa's question sounds more like a reproach than a *don't worry friend, I'll tell you why*. Looking at the faces of the others, she realises that her comment is not appropriate.

"Sorry!" She begins, as she looks down on the ground in apology. "The child is looking up at the Torre Nueva (the New Tower)."

I remember someone telling me something about that, but I can't remember what it is.

"The New Tower was the first great building built in Zaragoza in the 16th century. It was one of the most beautiful

Mudéjar towers. It had a great clock and, with its big bells, it alerted people of danger and it was used for normal everyday things."

Elsa stands up and motions us to follow her. I don't mind following her because I can't remember what she was saying.

She stops and, with her finger on the ground, draws a circle around it.

"Do you see these shapes on the ground?"

"Which one?" asks David.

It's true. There are several shapes all within each other.

If anyone was looking at us, they would be laughing at the five of us standing, looking down at the ground, each one in our own corner, following the various shapes.

"They are octagonal," Elsa continues. "They represent the base of the tower and its various levels which all had the same shape."

I had no idea.

"But they had to knock it down," Elsa continues "Several years after its construction, it began to lean, and by the end of the 19th century, the Council decided that they had to prevent the risk to the surrounding buildings."

Elsa stops midway as the rest of us look at the shapes.

"To commemorate the tower, which was very popular with the people in the city, they drew an octagon here where the tower was originally located, and put the statue of the boy you see here," she pointed at the place where we were sitting earlier, "looking up to the top of it."

"Wow!" David exclaims. "The number of times I have been here. I didn't have the faintest idea."

Elsa must have been feeling proud of herself because we are all looking at her. With the light grey long coat she's wearing today and the woollen cap with an equally grey visor, she has the romantic air of a poet. The only thing left for her to do is to recite a poem aloud for people to applaud.

"You haven't told the whole story." Samuel interrupts the almost magical moment.

Elsa looks at him a little seriously and the rest of us look at each other inquiringly.

"This is one of the examples that went against the balance of the city."

Samuel's last words are like a splash of cold water. For several days we've been talking about the balance in the city, even from Roman times, and now it looks as if there is something that's not right.

"You will say that!" Elsa exclaims a little rudely.

"The only thing I know," Samuel continues, "is that it is all shrouded in mystery. How could a 81-metre tower be built and be a ruin seven years later? If it was leaning during its construction, shouldn't they have had to stop works and rebuild it from the foundations up, or change the site if the subsoil did not support the right foundation? These are some of the questions I had heard."

Samuel moves towards the corner of El Temple Street. We follow him and, as we reach him, he invites us to look up.

There's a great painting on the facade of a wall, as high as the four-storey building on which it was painted. It is a representation of what the tower was like before it was thrown down. It's pretty.

An icy wind suddenly picks up and I have to gather my coat about me.

"It's getting late," David interrupts the moment. "With all that has happened in the ice cream shop and the commotion on Alfonso Street, time has flown and we haven't done what we had planned. I told my mother that I would be home within a half an hour."

"OK," I respond. "We'll return tomorrow afternoon if that's alright."

"Yes," Elsa and Erik agree simultaneously.

Samuel nods and, with that, he understood that he had said all that he needed to say.

Suddenly, David surprises us when he whispers:

"Have you seen who's outside that newspaper shop?"

"The man in the ice cream shop!" Erik responds, a little unsettled.

He's looking at the shop window with the little girl standing next to him and the pram with the baby. The mother must be inside.

"Do you see the mother?" David surprises me with his question.

"She must be buying something inside," I answer, as if it's obvious.

"No," David turns around, looking at me as if I had said something he had not expected me to say. "I would not have asked if I had seen her inside."

I don't know who's less diplomatic: me for implying that it should be obvious or him for his comment on implied stupidity.

Suddenly, I feel someone touch me from behind.

I turn around and my heart almost stops. Standing in front of me is the woman; the same woman who tried in vain to soothe the baby at the ice cream shop; the same woman who followed her husband in silence and glanced at me as she was leaving. She is no more than 5 feet tall, with long black hair, very dark eyes, aquiline nose and very pronounced cheekbones. She's pretty, but looks very tired, almost worn out. I look directly into her eyes. For some reason that I can't understand, I feel sure of myself at her side.

"Get away from here." She takes me by the arm and draws me a couple of metres away from where we were standing.

"Why?" I ask, although I don't put up any resistance to moving.

"It no longer matters," was the only answer I receive.

I don't understand what's happening. We've only moved a little. I look down at the ground and the only thing we've done is to move away from the lines of the octagon that were drawn on the ground. I look at her again and frown. I hope she understands that I think that what she's just done is absurd.

"I saw how you watched my daughter's pendant earlier," She tells me, with her eyes staring into mine, without taking notice of my alarm.

I don't know what to say. The others realise what's happening and are observing us in silence. I can't break my gaze.

A gust of wind makes her lift her left hand to flick her dark hair, blocking her view, from her face.

"I don't know what you know," she continues very seriously, "but I advise you to forget it and do not even try to find out more."

"Why are you saying this?" I ask her, now unsettled and unable to control my reaction.

She remains silent. She looks at my friends behind me and, aware that I'm following all her gestures, she takes out something from under her blouse with her right hand. Boldly, I look down and recognise that it is the same pendant with the same symbol the guide at the museum had given me. I can feel my eyebrows raising, my eyes opening wide and my jaw dropping.

"It's very dangerous. Leave now while you can."

Then, she walks away heading to the shop where her husband and children are standing, and points out our position to him. They look at us and the four of them hurry away along Torre Nueva Street towards the Central Market.

As we gaze after them, we can see two women collapsed on the ground, holding their ears.

CHAPTER 12

Friday 16 December 2016
Time: 3:30 pm

David

"Who's answering the phone?"

I am already at home. The first thing I hear is my mother calling out from her room. The house telephone can be heard everywhere. I look in the living room. My brother isn't there. The door to his room is ajar, but the light is off. I see that the door to the bathroom is closed. I go directly to the telephone. When the telephone has been ringing for a while, it is truly annoying. When I finish the call, I will change the ring tone. This reminds me of the unpleasant sound they used at my school to mark the end of break when I was little. How irritating! After such a good time on the patio to go back into class! I've always wondered why they don't have classes on the patio instead of the classrooms.

"I'll answer it, mum." I shout as I reach the phone.

Seeing what's next to the telephone as I pick up the telephone receiver, I shout:

"Your mobile's also here, if you are looking for it!"

"Thank you." I hear my mother call out from the back.

I turn my attention to the telephone receiver to find out who's calling. For a second, my heart skips a beat when I hear a female voice at the other end, saying:

"Is your mobile turned off? I've been trying to call you for some time."

Although not the same female voice that brightened my whole afternoon earlier, I'm very happy to hear Elsa's voice.

"I'm not sure," I answer, as I look at my phone. "Now I see what's happened. I must have put it on silent mode at some point and have not activated it again. How are you, Elsa?"

"I'm OK. I'm OK," she begins in an agitated voice. I've never heard her like this before. She always appears to be the epitome of the strong woman you see in the films, who's always keeping her emotions in check. Today, she's not, nor is she now. I begin to feel worried too. She then continues: "I have to tell you what's happened to me."

Her voice appears more relaxed. I become attentive. She manages to grab my attention:

"When I got home last night, the five of us sat down to dinner. I was distracted during dinner as I was thinking about what had happened to us up to this precise moment, going over everything step by step. I was a little worried..."

She stops for a moment as if taking a run-up to continue to release all that she wants to say to me in less than a minute.

".. Then I realised that the rest of my family were all very nice. My brothers only talked about the basketball match they had played that afternoon and my father could not stop telling us all how well his boys had played. I don't exactly know why, but I was surprised because lately, dinners tended to end up in arguments between my two older brothers. As I am the youngest, they always throw the blame on me and I end up going to bed angry with them."

For a moment, I can imagine the scene. I know she is the youngest. Not only is she the youngest, she is also the smallest in size. And as everything in life depends on your perspective, if we who are her companions think that she is big, her brothers are positively enormous. They have taken after their parents, both of whom are over 6 feet tall. What makes me laugh is the thought of that family of five having dinner in such a small kitchen as theirs is. Elsa always says that they wanted to move into another apartment because of the size of the kitchen. But they have never done so. The scene at least is amusing.

"During that moment of peace," Elsa continues, "I told them about all that had happened to us during the day and the story about the teacher and, in particular, what had happened at the museum."

She is quiet for a moment. Then, the tone of her voice changes as if she is angry:

"My brothers are such idiots!" She is upset and she knows it. She lowers her voice: "They laughed at me and would not let me continue talking! Can you believe it? But what was worse was that my father said: 'That's rubbish. You have to focus on studying what's really important, and all that story about the Romans and the city of Zaragoza is worthless. I've never learnt anything about that and look how well I've turned out. I've never needed all that nonsense'."

She falls quiet again. I ask her to continue because I don't know if she's going to cry or shout:

"It's my dad, for crying out loud, and I know that I'm important to him. If he knew how bad his words were going to make me feel, I am sure that he wouldn't have said it."

She stops for a moment and continues more calmly:

"I looked at him very sternly, I looked away and continued eating in silence. He will never know how close he came to getting all the wine in his glass spilt all over him 'accidentally' by me as I bumped against the table 'by accident'. But, you know David, they don't understand us. So once again, I let it pass."

Fortunately, no crying or shouting. But I am intrigued. From the little I know of Elsa, I know she would never call me just to tell me that.

"Has anything else happened, Elsa?"

"Yes, yes, that's why I called you," she continues. "Just as my father finished talking his rubbish, both my mother and father put their hands up in pain to cover their right ear at the same time. I remembered what had happened to the History teacher."

She remains quiet for a moment and sighs deeply.

"At that precise moment, they each received a text message on their mobiles. As it all felt so strange, although we keep our mobiles away from the table when we are eating, they both got up and picked up theirs."

At the other end, Elsa falls silent for a moment, but I can't contain myself:

"And what happened? Did they faint?" I ask.

"No, no. The earache didn't last long and I watched to see if they were bleeding. But they were not. They checked their messages and they read it at the same time having realised that their message was the same. It was only one sentence with the words joined up: "'Zaragozacollapses'.

I am quiet but intrigued. I see that my mother's mobile has an intermittent light flashing, indicating that there's a new text message.

"On reflex, I looked at my own mobile and saw that there were no messages," Elsa continues, rousing me from my distraction. Then, she asks, "Could you tell me if you've received a message?"

CHAPTER 13

Monday 19 December 2016
Time: 3:00 pm

Sofia

It's almost lunch time and, normally after school, we go home immediately as we would have been up from very early and would be hungry by this time. But today, the five of us have stayed chatting at the school gate to talk about what we did at the weekend. The problem is that we can't stop talking about what happened last week to many adults we know. They – Elsa's parents, David's mother and my mother – had all received the message. Samuel did not mention anything about his parents. He hasn't ever talked about them. It's strange that Erik's hadn't received a message, but the other parents of our classmates most certainly did. Apart from Samuel, the other students seem worried. I'm not, but I want to know what is going on.

As none of us believe in coincidences, we have been discussing the link between the text message and what we saw in the street over recent days with people losing their balance and falling over. I don't want to believe in strange things, but nothing about this is normal. I'm sure there is some logical explanation.

Next to me, Erik is pointing at the tablet in his hand. I give him a nudge, prompting him to suggest:

"Why don't we check on the Internet?"

He plonks himself down on the street, leaning back against the school wall and types in "Zaragozacollapses" on the search engine.

We are all surprised when we discover that the search engine has only found one website. We click on it and a photo appears showing an area in the city where the *Cardus* and *Decumanus* are clearly marked. As he passes the mouse across the screen, at the intersection of the two streets, there is a link to another webpage. He clicks on it and a new page opens up with a message:

"ZARAGOZA COLLAPSES, YOU KNOW WHAT YOU HAVE TO DO."

Under the text, there is the same symbol as on the note the guide at the museum gave me.

My mind is a whirl with ideas, but I can only say one thing:

"There's nothing more to say here! Let's do what they have suggested. Shall we meet up at 4 o'clock in the centre, opposite the Old Courts, next to the La Hispanidad fountain? I'm going home to drop off my books."

"Well, see you soon," David says goodbye as he heads home.

Erik smiles as he goes off in the opposite direction to his home. Samuel, as always, disappears without saying a word. I notice Elsa following me. This is unusual because she lives in the other direction.

How cold it is! An icy wind has picked up and I feel cold to my bones. As I put up the collar of my coat with my left hand, I hold my backpack with my books in the other. Then, I adjust the other side of my collar with my right hand. Elsa is also wearing her coat. As she is carrying her backpack on her shoulder, she has her hands free to put up the lapels of her coat. Walking on this side of the Huerva River is like walking through a wind tunnel. Having the fewest buildings, it gives the wind clear passage up to the Gran Vía Boulevard. Around us, also cloaked in overcoats and jackets buttoned up to the neck, people walk bent over against the force of the wind which is enough to throw you off-balance if you aren't bending forward.

"You're very quiet, Elsa." I try to break the ice as I watch her.

She is walking close to the stone wall to avoid falling into the river. She is so tall that I have to look up to see her eyes. She is very elegant. Her dark skin, offset by the white woollen cap she's been wearing since this morning and the beige coat reaching down to her knees, could very well get her onto the catwalk. She is a very good friend. We tell each other almost everything and what I like most about her is her concern for others. She is one of the few people I know who is more interested in seeing people other than herself having a good time.

"How was the chess championship on Saturday?"

I had almost forgotten. She is waiting to hear all the details.

"It was good because all the teams in the city were competing."

Since my parents signed me up to play chess five years ago, I haven't missed a single competition. It's not that I am very good, but I enjoy it. As I look at the 32 pieces on the white and black squares, I move them about in my head in various combinations for the next game. This makes me feel out of this world. Match times are good to make you disconnect and reconnect at the same time to a world in space, where you can see from a distance the pieces moving, as you calculate and remove each other's pieces. I absolutely love it.

Elsa turns to look at me from her height waiting for me to answer.

"We lost again," I replied. "The games were fast with the timer. I don't handle that very well. I like having as much time as possible to consider each move and having a clock at my side telling me that time is up makes me nervous." I dodge to avoid a plastic bag that someone had dropped. It was coming straight at my face. "Next Friday is the final and it is untimed. So, I think we will win. In the accumulated scores in the competitions this year, we are in the lead."

"That's great." Elsa smiles in response. "That's optimism for you!"

We are already at the intersection with Gran Via Boulevard. It is less windy here because of the buildings providing protection.

"Did you go out on Saturday?" Elsa asks.

"The games finished at 7 p.m. and our whole team went out for dinner."

"Did you go alone?" Elsa's question takes me aback.

"No, Erik came to meet me." I don't understand what she's getting at. "Why do you ask?"

Some mothers with small children crossing the street almost knock us over. The kids have escaped from them and are now running to the swings in the centre of the boulevard. There are no cars or trams passing, but what a fright they have given us.

Elsa does not answer. So, I stop. She has not realised and continues walking until she recognises that I am no longer walking alongside. She stops and turns back to look at me. I walk two steps towards her and, looking directly at her, I wait for her to answer.

"Sofia, I am very happy for you." As Elsa starts, I know I'm not going to like what she's going to say next. "But," here it comes, "You must know that ever since you started going out with Erik, you have hardly called me."

Ah, so that was it. What was her problem?

I didn't want this to be happening. Deep down, I didn't want to go out with any boy precisely for this reason. I didn't want to stop being with my friends and, even less, having *them* tell me this. What's more, she's right. On Saturday, with the chess championship and then the dinner, I had forgotten to call her. Then, on Sunday I spent almost the whole day studying and, in the afternoon, Erik and I went out for a walk. It had never even occurred to me to call her. I feel super guilty.

"You are right." I look at her as we continue standing together. "It will not happen again."

"I didn't say this to you for you to apologise. I only want us to continue to be friends and to go out together occasionally. I know that it's not the same."

We exchange smiles and continued walking.

"For sure," I respond in the air, "and how's it with David?"

"What?!" She responds, almost angrily.

"Sorry, sorry." I have to calm her down because I seem to have offended her. "As I see you together in class, you chat a lot..."

For a moment, there is a break in the clouds and a ray of light shines directly down on us. It is like being in a film. It is deceptive, since it is just as cold as ever, less windy here, but cold all the same.

"I know he is a very good person, handsome and I like him." Elsa responds, looking down on the ground, "but his heart is with someone else."

CHAPTER 14

Monday 19 December 2016
Time: 4:00 pm

David

I observe my four companions as we walk through the centre of Plaza del Pilar. It is impressive. Each time I come here, I enjoy looking up to admire the whole scene from the great fountain. I like entering the plaza from the area of the Old Courts, more than from any of the other streets.

I take in the fountain and the sculptures in this part of the plaza.

The fountain represents the map of South America and the large globe, the world as it was before Christopher Columbus left on his voyage of Discovery. That I understand. But those three walls representing the three caravels he used to cross the Atlantic, that's too much for my imagination.

In any case, and from the photos of the past that I've seen, I'd say that I've always liked this plaza, then as now. I can't remember exactly when it changed. I'd say that there were two occasions: the first was when they remodelled the plaza and installed these large lights; the other was after the World Fair in 2008, when they cleaned the towers of the Basilica. The best thing about this plaza is the great open space, often used to hold large crowds of people, especially during festival times in the city.

I have great memories of this place. When I was small, I used to play with my parents and my brother with the water in the little, round fountains near the entrance of the Basilica. What I enjoyed most was when my mother managed to get the pigeons – and there were hundreds of them – to eat out of her hand. She was thrilled. I had always pictured myself getting all of them to eat from *my* hand. My parents would be proudly watching me. Everyone in the plaza would be talking about me.

But I never could, because I was incapable of keeping still for a minute without fidgeting, and of course, that would scare the birds away.

The pigeons must be hiding today because I can't see any of them. It's an unpleasant day to go for a walk. There is a strong freezing wind and we are practically alone in the plaza. Both birds and people must have thought that it wasn't a good afternoon to be out like this... Only us, and only because we have a very specific aim.

"What did they tell you at home when you said that you weren't going to have lunch?" Erik asks us.

"They didn't give me any hassle." Elsa replied, "but I mentioned that I was going to do a project with you all."

"At least, *you* didn't lie to them." I interrupt her. "We *are* going to do a project."

"I had a bit of a problem because, since my father's disappearance, my mum, brother, sister and I have always eaten together," Sofia remarks. "It was a bit awkward because my mother, in fact, didn't say a word. She simply went quiet." There is a pause. "That's worse."

Erik goes to her, puts his hand on her shoulder and draws her towards him. She rests her head against him. I can't stand it. I turn away.

That's the other reason why I feel so close to her. We were both left without our fathers. For me, it happened many years ago, but for her, it's been less than a year now. I've only just realised that, this time, I'm not thinking about Erik's gesture of affection in holding her, but in how Sofia must be feeling. How I would love to tell her how much I feel for her! How I would love to console her at this moment because I've already gone through it! But I am churning away at something which is crushing me from inside. And it is pointless. I'm going to have to put a stop to this.

We are heading for the address the guide at the museum had given to Sofia. I look at the building on my left. It's the La Lonja building. To break the silence, Sofia remarks:

"I've always thought this building impressive. The details at the top with faces embedded on the facade and along the external walls are very interesting, mainly because I've never understood what they stand for."

As we pass near the building, Elsa points north where we could see the stone bridge over the Ebro.

"Look! The northern gate to the city must have been there. There is nothing there now, but the other day, I saw in a book that it was called the Angel Gate, and there was a sculpture above the entrance."

"Better not mention what really happened at the gate." Samuel suggests.

"Why do you say that?" Elsa inquires, looking at him in surprise.

With a look of disgust on his face and in a low voice, he explains, "For years, they left the bodies of crooks and criminals executed in the city hanging for months so that everyone entering the city could see and know what they did in Zaragoza."

The girls look like they are going to be sick. Erik and I look at each other knowingly, and shrug our shoulders.

As we continue walking, we look to our left towards the old Angel Gate.

Pointing at the stone bridge, Samuel continues, "The worst was when they executed the Lord Chancellor of Aragon in 1592, soon after Castilian troops occupied the city. They left his body hanging for seven years until 1599 when Philip III visited."

"How barbaric!" Elsa exclaimed. "How disgusting! How could they do that?"

What a history! It would only occur to Samuel to tell a story like that? That boy only seems to know about gruesome things.

Erik has only just discovered that he does not like history after all. I notice him stopping just as we pass in front of the Cathedral of San Salvador, also called La Seo, making us turn to look at him:

"By the way, changing the subject," he starts, "my parents did not get a text message on 'Zaragozacollapses', but all the parents of our classmates that I have asked received one."

I look at Samuel, on my right, to see if he was going to take the opportunity to give us the information he hadn't wanted to disclose earlier. But it's clear that this boy only speaks when he wants to. We will never know if his parents received the same message or not. We will never really know anything about his parents. He just resumes walking in his own customary style in which even his shoulders also seem to be walking, one forward and then back, and then the other and so on. He doesn't even look at us.

Sofia pipes up:

"Actually, I asked the teachers this morning, and they also received a message. It's very odd."

"Well, I think it's a marketing campaign," I add. I manage to grab Sofia's attention. "I'm sure that they have commissioned some company to run a new ad campaign to promote the city."

"Well, they must be doing a really good job," she responds.

"Why do you say that?" Elsa inquires, turning to her.

"Because lots of people are talking about Zaragoza," Sofia responds. "The message you are talking about, everyone who's received it has sent it on to someone else because it looked so interesting. It's gone viral."

"It is worse than that. You are not going to believe it," Erik suddenly interrupts, looking at his tablet. He then walks over to sit down on the benches at the bus stop nearby.

Following him, we sit down next to him as he shows us his screen, saying:

"This marketing company must be very good because here it is in Spanish, French and Italian. Look, if you type in 'Zaragozasedesploma', the search engine goes to a single page and it is the same we've seen before. It's the same if you type in 'Zaragozasécroule' in French, and 'Zaragozacollassara' in Italian."

"They are good!" Elsa exclaims admiringly. "But... who are they?"

"That's the oddest thing," replies Erik. "They have not said and I can't find any information about them. I have sat down to try to trace the source... but there is no way." He points at the screen and says, "Look, if you go to this webpage, it tells you who the owner of the website is. I have done it and some details come up, but then I cannot go to the source."

I know what he is talking about because at the end of the last school year, we had to do an Internet project. They had explained all the tricks about how to create a webpage, how to register a domain and how things had developed in recent years. Each group had to do an example. I was amazed at how easy it was, but what Erik is talking about rings true. It ought to be easy to find out who is behind that URL address because they have to have it registered in some server. They had explained that there were people who registered in the name of a company based in countries far away so that they could not be found. Then, you would discover that it was the property of another based in Europe, and so you would have to trace the original. In the work that we did, we always found the source. But not today.

"It's good that they think it's mysterious. That's good for the city. More publicity. Let's get back to the business in hand." I try to end the chat, mainly because it revolves around Erik.

Sofia looks at me because the man also sitting on the bench has just lost his balance. Moreover, he appears to be asleep with his head slumped onto her shoulder. With a gesture of disgust, she moves away from the man who literally collapses onto the bench with only his legs sticking out from under him. When she pulls herself together, as if nothing has happened, she says:

"Yes, it's strange that none of us have received a message, nor anyone of our age group..." She falls silent for a moment.

"Nor Erik's parents. Normally when something is sent out to one of us, we always get wind of it."

"In any case, let's not get sidetracked from what's important," Elsa interrupts her, pointing at the man who has just moved away. "People are falling over in the street and that's not our imagination. In the short time we've been walking through this plaza, I've seen at least four people, without counting this one," she points to the body next to her.

We get up from the bench, and walk along Don Jaime Street towards our destination, looking around us in silence. Everywhere we look, it is the same: people losing their balance and collapsing all over the place.

As we pass by a newsagent's, I go up to the window, look in and gesture to the others. Dumbly, I point at the front page of the main newspaper of the city. The headline on the front page is plain for everyone to see: 'ZARAGOZA COLLAPSES'. I can't resist and buy a copy.

Out of the blue, I get not what I was expecting, but what I was yearning for.

Pressed against me, she reads the front page with me. I can hardly read. I think it is the first time she has been so close. Unintentionally, her breasts are pressed against my arm. I am imagining so many things that I try not to think about. Erik and Elsa ask what is in the newspaper. In a low voice, we quickly read, almost in unison, the third paragraph of the article. Actually, we begin to read and then stop immediately when we realise that we have started at the same time with the exactly the same thing. We look at each other for a second. She smiles at me. I quickly fall quiet, allowing her to carry on reading:

After a spate of people collapsing in the street, the town council have been forced to organise a recovery team to pick up the people affected and take them to their homes until they are able to ascertain what has been happening. Some are so disoriented that they are unable to speak. The main problem confronting the Council is that some people have remained in such a state and either do not have sufficient documentation, or at the address that they have for them, there is no one there, or no one answers the door.

She stops, looks at me for a moment and I alone continue reading:

All adults in Zaragoza are advised to carry sufficient documentation when they go out so that, if necessary, the authorities can verify where they live. If using a mobile phone, people are advised to put at the top of the saved list of contact telephone numbers the emergency contact number of the person they want the authorities to contact, should they need assistance.

I stop reading, look at Sofia and, without being conscious of it, we read the last line together at the same time:

The Council says that there is no need for alarm and recommends that all citizens continue life as normal.

When we finish and look up at Erik and Elsa's faces, I can't decide which of them is more astonished. The two of them looking at us as we read looked as if they were turned to stone.

Standing on the pavement, Samuel turns in the direction we are going.

"It's strange," he remarks, "there's no one on the ground on this street."

We look around. He's right! Since we turned onto the Plaza de La Seo at Don Jaime Street, no one appears to have any problem standing up.

Erik stops staring at us. He looks at a clock calendar nearby, on which today's date can be seen.

CHAPTER 15

Monday 19 December 2016
Time: 4:30 pm

Sofia

Walking along Don Jaime Street can be a bit tricky at some
points of the day. According to my parents, it was good that the
street was paved with cobbles, which gave this part of the city
an older look. So, it was a shame that a few years ago, they
removed all the cobble stones and replaced them with an
asphalt surface. I liked the fact that they reduced traffic, or at
least that's what they said at the time. The problem is that the
street is so narrow that there is only one lane for vehicles. So,
between taxis and buses, it is often blocked, especially because
the pavements are normally packed with people. Pedestrians
cross the street where there are no traffic lights and cause
chaos.

Today is one of those days. Compared to the Plaza del Pilar,
the street is absolutely overflowing with people and cars. Since
I was a child, I have always enjoyed the shops here (there are
still some remaining) where they sell the traditional sweets of
the city and candied fruits with chocolate. When I wanted to
buy Maraschino cherries, my mother would always say, "Sofia,
don't touch those sweets. They have alcohol in them!" They are
my favourites. But as my mother said, they have some liqueur.
Anyway, at 16, no one can tell me anything and I can eat as
much as I like. The problem is that they are smothered in
chocolate and, at 16, I have a certain problem with chocolate. I
can never get the balance right with those sweets. "Perhaps,
later on," I tell myself repeatedly as we continue walking.

Fortunately, after the last part of the walk, we identify the
door on the street from the note the guide gave me. I look at the
door bell and then at the others. I reckon they are thinking the
same thing as I am. I don't know what to say. I have no idea

how to introduce ourselves. For a moment, we wait in silence, looking at the door bell until Erik steps forward and presses it. The rest of us look at him in astonishment. He, in turn, looks back and then shrugs his shoulders as if to say, "what else are we supposed to do?!"

After a while, there is a voice on the intercom:

"Who is it?"

It is a man's voice, not a young voice, but a deep one. We look at each other, not knowing what to say, until Erik responds rather quickly and nervously:

"They gave us a note with this address."

There is silence. Then the voice replies:

"Where did they give you the note?"

Silence! We look at each other until Elsa answers hesitantly:

"In the Provincial Museum."

Again, silence. Then the voice responds:

"Who gave it to you?"

David quickly answers:

"We can't say."

The rest of us look at him with a mixture of surprise and annoyance. I think he has just messed everything up with that response. Silently, we make our recriminations felt for what he has just done with hand signals. In the middle of this silent debate, the front door opens.

We stay absolutely quiet as we survey the interior. David, on the other hand, uses the opportunity to look at us and grin broadly.

Half pushing his way through, Samuel wends his way between us and is the first to cross the threshold and go up the steps. He only realises that we haven't moved by the time he climbs four steps. He wheels around and with a smile I have never seen before, he shrugs his shoulders. Then, like a little child wanting to be first, he hurries up the stairs. Without looking at each other, but knowing that each of us has a smile on our faces, we follow him.

We go up the steps until we reach the house. The door is open. From inside, we can hear the voice of an older man:

"Come in, come in. I know why you have come."

CHAPTER 16

Monday 19 December 2016
Time: 5:00 pm

David

Although my family live far from the city centre, on occasion we have visited friends of my parents who live in this sector. Almost all the floors were quite dark and filled with old furniture. I didn't know what we might find in this house we were going to visit. I look at Sofia and then at the others. I can see we are all equally expectant.

The room is not very big. I would say that it is like a square with sides measuring 4 metres in length. It was big enough to accommodate a large four seater sofa and a dining table with six chairs around it. Next to the living room-diner, there is a kitchen and an office annexed to it. You can see that someone was cooking a short time ago. What surprises me most as I sit with the others and the man around the table is that everything is decorated in white: not only the walls, or the covering of the sofa, the tables and chairs, but also the floor.

We are all waiting. The man appears to be old, and quite tired. Yet, he has a penetrating gaze, which creates a certain air of mystery about him. He is covered from head to toe in a white tunic except for a pair of black boots he is wearing. Although a little hidden, mainly because of the hood over his head, I can make out that his hair is white and his sharp eyes a sky blue. I estimate that he must be in his seventies. Despite his wrinkled skin, I can see he looks after himself very well.

The man breaks the silence as he watches us:

"Do you know why you have come?"

We look at each other and nod. Sofia explains:

"Because they have given us a note with your address."

The man speaks again, but this time with a slight smile:

"I am referring to the real reason for you coming here."

Sofia looks at us. I don't know how to respond or how to help her out. No one else says anything. Meanwhile, Samuel is looking around him, shamelessly inspecting every corner of the room, as if the conversation does not interest him. Erik and Elsa keep looking directly at the man. Sofia is rubbing her eyes as she always does when she is nervous. I am wondering how could the surface of the table be so white, without a mark, scratch or anything to indicate it has ever been used.

The man manages to surprise us when he stands up abruptly, moving his chair back and announcing:

"In that case, I cannot help you. Have a good day. Please close the door when you leave." He goes to the window, pulls the curtain back and starts looking at the people walking on the street below.

After inviting us in, is he dismissing us already? What kind of stupidity is this?! This guy is mad! I look at his face. Sofia is the most surprised of us all. She looks uncomfortable, as if angry and about to explode. I have no wish to see her in a temper. In fact, she is the first to stand up, ready to leave. The rest of us do the same and follow her out.

As we are walking towards the exit, Sofia who clearly does not want to waste this meeting because at the end of the day we are here because of her, turns around, walks up to the man, shows him the note and, pointing to the rectangle drawn on it below, says:

"We have come because I asked a question and I was given a piece of a paper with this drawing."

She falls silent as she holds out her hand with the folded paper for him to see.

It was almost ludicrous: Sofia standing while the rest of us are about to leave.

No. Not all of us.

I suddenly notice that Samuel has not even moved from his chair. In fact, he is at the table, typing something on his tablet.

The man turns away from the window, looks at the drawing, opens his eyes wide, then looks at Sofia, and with a slight twist of his head, raises his eyebrows.

Sofia regards him and says:

"I know what the rectangle is..."

The man quietly turns to look at Samuel who has stopped taking notes and is now holding the old man's gaze. The freak shrugs his shoulders and gives one of his strange smiles. I say 'strange' because I can't work out what he means by it.

At last, the man turns back to Sofia and looks at her closely. Smiling broadly at us, he motions for us to sit down again. Samuel smiles at each of us.

It is only when we sit down that Sofia finishes her sentence:

"... but I don't know what the rest means."

The man scrutinises us and, after sitting down again, says:

"Good afternoon, my name is Nicola. I am going to explain it to you.

CHAPTER 17

Monday 19 December 2016
Time: 6:00 pm

Sofia

Normally, young boys on skateboards practise their new moves near the entrance of the Cathedral of the Saviour (La Seo) and next to the entrance of the old Roman forum. They use the slope for their jumps and use the steps near the fountain to try out their spins. Today, there is no one here because of the cold. The sun continues shining, but the wind makes it bitterly cold at this time of year.

According to my mother, the Plaza de la Seo was different before. It seemed smaller, with a pedestrianised area in the city centre, and surrounded by a street to accommodate traffic. The most notable feature in the plaza are the trees which are very welcome on hot summer days when temperatures rise to over 40 degrees. Nowadays, as I all too well know, there is no shade whatsoever. This plaza is a continuation of the great airy space of the adjacent Plaza del Pilar. Basically, it is like an extension of the other, although there are various different levels on the ground. Some steps go up 20 cm in threes, parallel to Don Jaime Street, then drop five more to the level of the plaza. Mostly, they are used as places for people to sit.

The fountain's water surface extends to the tall monument in the middle of the plaza and the steps used for seating run along the entire length of the fountain. At 20 metres in height, there are three sheer rectangular walls covered in huge light brown tiles and erected to touch each other along their shorter sides. Just beneath, there is a sign indicating the entrance to the Roman Forum.

Among the four sides of the plaza, one is Don Jaime I Street and another is a three-storey building painted in ochre which stands out against the white facade of the chapel adjoining the

Cathedral of the Saviour on the opposite side of the street. The main entrance to the Cathedral is finished in the same colour of the dark brick of the rest of the church. I feel so tiny next to this building and the enormous monument.

When the weather is good, there are quite a lot of people milling around, but not today.

Taking advantage of the fountain steps being empty and there is no one in the plaza, I sit down first, but near ground level for protection against the wind. I spread out flat the large map of the city of Zaragoza given to us a few minutes earlier at the Tourist Office, after we left Nicola's house.

Erik who, for some time has not made any attempt to hold my hand, looks at me in silence. He then mechanically superimposes on the map a transparency that Elsa has purchased in the shop on the corner. On it we draw the rectangle with the lines the guide at the museum had given us, but to scale.

Don't ask me how, but Samuel produces a small ruler, a set square and a protractor from his pockets. He sure is unpredictable, never ceasing to amaze me.

Looking on, Elsa says:

"That is exactly what Nicola told us to do - to put the rectangle on the map of Zaragoza."

David stoops down to see it in detail and exclaims:

"It's incredible! How they match! Just by shifting the *Cardus* and the *Decumanus* and the rectangle."

The wind abates a little, but the cold is as intense as ever. The grey clouds floating across the sky above us indicate that it is going to rain soon. No one notices us, not because of a lack of interest, but because the place is deserted. Quite literally we have the plaza to ourselves. I love that.

As they all observe the map, I am able to get a look at David, and see how good his fringe looks on him and how attractive he is today. I suppose that all rowers have bodies as fit as his. I don't reckon he has an ounce of extra fat on him. Today, he has been particularly nice... but why am I looking at him? Erik also looks very handsome today. What is happening to me? David is just my friend and Erik is my boyfriend. That's all! Let's get back to the task in hand.

"And we can see the four gates to the city and the corners," I comment. "It is clear that it is not lined up with the north."

"Then,' says Erik, without looking at me, "it is as Nicola has said. The drawing they gave you is a solstice rectangle."

By using the rectangle on the drawing he is holding, he indicates the various directions of the setting and the rising of the sun at the different solstices and equinoxes. According to Nicola, the outline of the Roman city walls is drawn within the boundaries of the rectangle, the proportions of which are not arbitrary since they maintain proportionality between its sides, which are linked to the latitude of the city of Zaragoza.

I recognise that, until a few hours ago at Nicola's house, no one had ever heard of a 'solstice rectangle'. I don't know what to think. Fortunately, Erik seeing our blank faces when the rectangle was mentioned, is now reading out the explanation from the Internet on his tablet:

The solstice rectangle has a specific proportion determined by the orientation of the sunrise at the summer solstice. With regard to the north, this angle, called the *azimuth*, differs in latitude to the one we find ourselves in now, which requires the orientation to be calculated by the shadow created by the vertical pole on that solar day. Once the shadow had been marked, a circle was drawn. The intersection of the shadow on the circle defined the rectangle that was inscribed in the circle, with its diagonal corresponding with the shadow....

We watch him slide his finger across the screen from the bottom to the top to continue reading the text:

This geometrical pattern was fundamental in creating any sacred construction, and was used by all cultures.

"Impressive!" I exclaim. "I had no idea."

The others are silent, but from their faces, I can glean that the identical thought must have occurred to them at the same time as me. I am beginning to enjoy this more and more. We seem to be opening a door to a room that we have not entered before. And the woman at the ice-cream parlour? What do I do with the information she gave me later in the Plaza San Felipe? Danger? I don't want to believe it. But, her eyes... There was an unfathomable depth within that look. And what the guard at the museum said to Elsa. How could I forget it?

"It is the second time that the mention of a *sacred city* has come up, and now a *sacred construction*," David points out. I focus back on the conversation.

"And so, by rotating it a little," Elsa suggests as she moves the transparency with the rectangle on top of the map. "The *Cardus* and the *Decumanus* of the two streets coincide."

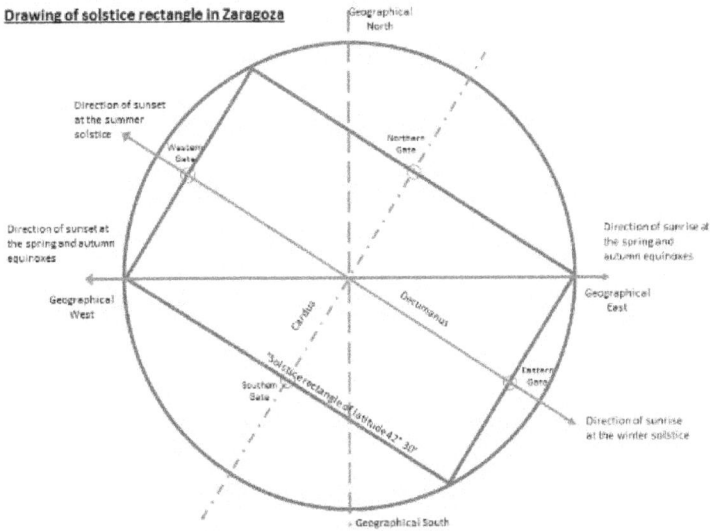

Drawing of solstice rectangle in Zaragoza

David and Elsa exclaim at the same time:

"The alignment is mind-blowing! Nicola was right!"

We remain silent, all observing and turning the transparency around to check each of the orientations and alignments in turn.

Samuel stuns us all by saying, "And don't forget what the old man said."

The problem is that when he speaks, he does it so quickly and in such abrupt tones that I sometimes find it hard to understand him. He picks up his notepad and begins to read:

This rectangle is known in operational geometry as the 'solstice rectangle' and it has the power to harmonise the energies at the core of the Earth, commanding the four elements (fire, water, earth and air), in its four corners, and the fifth element, ether, at its centre.

Elsa stops looking at the map and stares at me:

"Why did you tell the old man that you knew what the rectangle was?"

There is a slight silence as my four friends stare at me. I feel as if I am being interrogated. But I am not bothered. I am about to answer. But I pause as the bells at the cathedral begin to ring. It is 7 pm.

"Because it is in the book that my father left open on the day he disappeared," I reply when, at last, the bells have stopped, and looking at the paper, I continue: "Since he never returned from his last expedition, my mother has never wanted to touch anything on his desk." I remain silent as I look at the map. "The disappearance of my father was a total shock for her. Just think about it, he went on some excavation in the north of Italy and then disappeared. He was never heard of again. That was what the authorities told my mother after searching for him for a month which they normally give for people who have disappeared. She sank into a deep depression for the next month. Then, suddenly she perked up, became more active at home again and started rearranging my father's things in all the rooms, all except in his office."

I don't think I have ever filled them in with so many details before. I feel relieved and above all, I feel listened to and cared for by my friends. Elsa is looking at me with so much tenderness that I could have hugged her there and then. I swallow hard before carrying on.

"As you can imagine," I continue, "because he was a researcher, his desk was always in a total mess. Apart from being a History professor at the University, he had various on-going research projects, and he left everything there on his desk. Don't ask me why. My mother does not want to touch

112

anything. She says that when one of her children grows up and learns about the same field, they might carry on his research. The truth is that I don't like History. I hope my brother or sister can realise my mother's dream."

I pause a while, only to confirm that they are listening. Then I continue:

"After I looked at the paper the guide at the museum gave me, I checked one of the books on my father's desk. It was open on page 23 with the same drawing on it. The name of the book was *The City of Zaragoza*, Nomenclarot, 1808."

As I have it with me today in my bag, I take it out in case anyone wants to leaf through it. Samuel practically snatches it from my hands and starts rifling through it.

"But for as much as I read, I still could not understand why it was on a tilt. I checked the internet and I saw that other cities in the world were built following the *Cardus* and *Decumanus* principle, but none of them were tilted. I'm sure that there must be one, but I couldn't find any, except this one: Caesaraugusta."

I feel a drop on my hand. Damn! It's beginning to rain. We quickly gather up the map and the rest of things we had laid out.

"There is only one more important thing we need to do: to verify the rest," David says as we try to run into the arcades.

Deep down, I am relieved by his comment. Otherwise, I would be the only crazy one here.

We keep on running.

Now, we are sheltering from the rain in the arcades just in front of the Las Palomas restaurant.

Erik spreads out the map once more on the ground and we cluster around him. Here, however, we've managed to attract some attention. A few passers-by have also sort shelter where we are waiting for it to stop raining. Curious to find out what we are doing, some come closer to look over our shoulders.

Fortunately, we have Samuel with us. With a couple of swear words, he manages to frighten them off. We look at each other, shrug our shoulders and focus on the map again.

Looking at us and adopting an attitude I have never seen before, Erik begins to take charge, arranging the maps and the papers, and says:

"Let's go over what we have. According to this, Don Jaime I Street is the *Cardus*, and the Calle Mayor, with Espoz and Mina streets further down, the *Decumanus*. We know where the four gates are: one opposite the Stone bridge, the other next to the Roman walls, the third is the entrance to El Tubo District, and the fourth is the Plaza de la Magdalena.

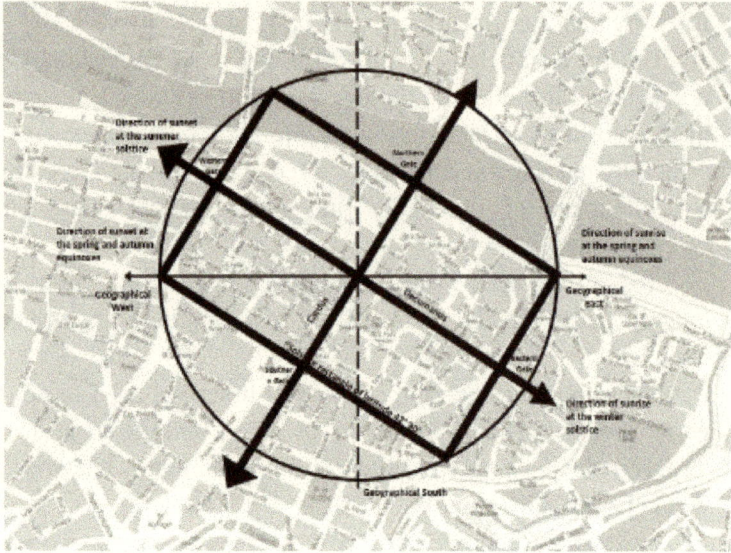

Elsa looks at him and then asks us:

"And this, what does this have to do with all the adults falling over?"

She manages to wipe the smile from our faces... all except Samuel's.

CHAPTER 18

Monday 19 December 2016
Time: 8:00 pm

David

As we enter Nicola's house, I realised that it is not the same as the last time we were there. He is wearing the same clothes: a long white tunic. However, this time, I notice a little figurine at the entrance into the house. I don't know what it is or what it represents. It is only a head of man. Actually, it's not that either. It is the head of a man with two faces, each of which is looking in the opposite direction. I am sure I've seen it before, but I can't recall where.

I noticed that Sofia has also noticed it. I am not surprised because there is something strange about her. Everything seems very orderly here.

Wow! I can't believe it! I make signs to the others, pointing at the symbol which is everywhere. It is the same tilted rectangle we saw on the paper the guide at the museum had given to Sofia. In the centre, there is a small symbol, but it is so small that I am not sure what it specifically represents. I am convinced that it was not here the other afternoon, but now it is, not only in the two pictures above the sofa, but also on the furniture under the window. It is on a small ornament, etched in relief on a piece of Roman stone placed on the furniture.

The city plan and the rectangles we made are spread out on the table.

After waiting for us all to be quiet, Sofia, standing next to Nicola, starts speaking:

"Nicola, we put the maps on top and did as you have instructed. After our chat this afternoon, we are now ready for you to tell us what the next step is."

I look at him a little sceptically.

My mind is full of contradictions. What are we doing here with an old man who we don't know and with something that is incredible, in the middle of an enormous problem in the city? It has never happened to me before. I would say this is only a dream. I like daydreaming to escape reality, but now, it's *déjà vu*, as if we have done this already and I will soon wake up.

After Sofia's statement, I notice Erik and Elsa waiting for the old man to respond. Samuel, on the other hand, is his usual quiet self. It's as if he's not here. However, this time I notice that, like me, he is looking around and studying every nook and cranny of the room. If he weren't human, I would say he is doing an electronic sweep of the room, trying to upload it onto his virtual memory.

As no one is saying anything, and without wanting to be too forward, I explain:

"All this mystery, with the guide at the museum giving us the paper and afterwards meeting you, has coincided with what is happening in Zaragoza."

I stop and look around the room.

"I notice that you do not have a television or computer and I have not seen a mobile telephone either. So, I don't know if you are aware of the message that Zaragoza is collapsing and people are fainting on the streets."

I fall silent. No one responds. You could cut the silence in the house with a knife.

"I knew that it would happen one day...", Nicola replied, attracting everyone's attention, including Samuel who, since we arrived, has not looked at him directly in the face.

We remain silent as we look at him, with eyes wide like saucers waiting for him to continue.

"...That's why I am here," he finishes.

As he said that, we look at each other. I don't know whether we are stunned into silence or thinking that he is just bonkers. What is true is that, ever since we met this man, we have proven that everything he has said is true, and none of us know who he is.

He stands up slowly, supporting himself with his hands on the table. He turns to face the window. All of us, including Samuel, gather around him to look out the window. The curtains are drawn back. There below, we can see the intersection between the streets. As we lift our gaze, on top of the building across the street, we can see the darkly-coloured weather vane, with the four points of the compass represented two levels below it. Today, there is a north-westerly wind blowing and the weather vane is oriented accordingly.

With the motion of his hand, he invites us to sit down around the table.

"You have already told me," he began, "that your teacher had explained why Emperor Augustus used the city as the one of the first cities on the Iberian Peninsula. Then, you are probably wondering why the Iberian Peninsula bears the name of the river which passes through our city."

We all nod in agreement.

"They have also explained to you that this was a sacred city for Rome."

We nod again, but this time I look around the house and, particularly, at the small figurine on the furniture at the entrance. A strange sensation runs through my whole body like a small electric shock.

"It must continue being a sacred city, but the problem is that someone is changing the order of things."

I can see Erik and Elsa raising their brows and smiling at the same time. Samuel starts taking notes again. I begin to feel uncomfortable. I begin to think that we are talking to a madman. However, when I glance at Sofia, I notice that she is totally engrossed in the conversation.

It is strange. I recall the woman in the ice cream shop and the daughter with the pendant of the symbol. We all saw her talking to Sofia. I don't know if Sofia has told us everything the woman had told her. Just the fact that she warned us that there is danger if we continue makes me shudder. Does it have anything to do with what Nicola is telling us now? In fact, I am

117

going to stop thinking about all this nonsense because it's overwhelming me. Let's see how he continues.

"You are very young, but if you ask your parents and grandparents who have lived here longer than you, they would confirm that Zaragoza has two features that few cities on the peninsula can put on their posters: wind and sun."

He stops for a moment to draw air, and continues:

"The wind and the sun, together with the geography of the area have endowed the people who live in Zaragoza, I don't mean the ones who were born here, but rather those who live here..." He stops for a moment, "...with some inner strength which, throughout history, has enabled them to do incredible things."

He begins to pace the room as if he wanted to walk around the table.

"Ask your teachers and parents, and find out how many people living in Zaragoza are knowledgeable of the significant feats, including how the city earned itself the title of *Very Noble*, *Very Loyal*, *Very Heroic* and *Very Benevolent*."

"That's on the coat of arms of the city," exclaims Elsa in a loud voice.

"So it is," responds Nicola. "Moreover, *persistence*, a characteristic attributed to the people of Zaragoza, is born out of the combination of wind, sun and something more."

We look at each other as the old man settles back into his chair.

"How can a person capable of adapting to such a severe, constantly changing and extreme climate not be persistent?"

He pauses for a moment and then continues:

"And what is this *something more*?" Nicola asks and looks out the window in silence. "The city founded by Rome was built by orienting the *Decumanus* according to the direction of the dominant wind, which we call the *cierzo*. In other words, it was assumed that, for sacred balance, this wind always had to enter through the Western Gate, and leave by the Eastern Gate."

He turns to look at us again. He watches as Erik returns to his seat, turns it around and now sits with his body and arms resting against the back. Samuel sits down on the armchair and continues to take notes on his tablet.

"Moreover, at sunset on the day spring turns into summer (the summer solstice) the Western Gate should be clearly lit up; similarly, sunrise on the day autumn turns into winter (winter solstice) should illuminate the Eastern Gate fully. It is part of the key to balance."

We again look at the table where Erik is turning the transparency with the geometrical drawings around on the map of the city for them to coincide, as we have discovered.

Elsa cannot contain what she is thinking:

"That's incredible! I think very few people in this city know it."

Sofia jumps up, exclaiming:

"How could the Romans calculate all this and build a whole city, following just a simple drawing?"

I watch the map again and say:

"So, on 23rd December, at dawn, the Church of La Magdalena should be fully illuminated..." It may be nonsense, but I will say it all the same. "Therefore, the plaza of the church is oriented like this for it not to block the sun?"

There is silence, until Nicola sits up on his seat at the table and says:

"You see?" he points at the map with his large fingers. "The wind enters here and should leave through there, and as you have explained it very well," he extends his right hand towards me, "at dawn of the winter solstice, the sun should be illuminating the church."

What he says makes sense, although it is all so strange. But, is it true? I look at the city plan and the street directions he is talking about. What he said about the Magdalena Church is impressive. I've passed by it many times. It is true that, for most of the time, it is bathed by the sun. However, how precise that a street starting at the entrance of the church should be oriented to the exact spot where the winter solstice dawns... How do we know that they did it for this purpose? It is one thing to discover a coincidence and another to discover that what you thought was a coincidence isn't, because it really was perfectly planned.

At this point, Sofia cuts through my thoughts:

"And what does this have to do with the adults losing their balance and falling over?"

Nicola turns towards her with a blank expression on his face. He looks at the rest of us and smiles. Then, he walks to the window again.

"Do you see that weather vane?" He waits for us to cluster around him to look through the window. "If you ask the people of Zaragoza whether they know that there is a weather vane just at the intersection of these two streets, what do you think they would say? Do you think that they would know about it?"

There are many people in the street. This weather vane dominates the junction, but I think that no one is aware of it. It is positioned directly facing the northwest. Before we entered Nicola's house, it had stopped raining and now the wind has picked up again. Clouds now cover the sun and it feels like a polar freeze out there. How grateful I am that we are indoors, even though the heating is lower than in our homes.

After a moment of silence, he continues:

"Very few people know about it. I think that practically no one does, except perhaps the person who put it there." He is silent for a moment, "And the watchman."

Sofia is astonished, but she seems incredulous now. Erik looks like someone who does not believe in any of this. Samuel, on the other hand, studies the map following who knows what with his gaze as he scribbles something down on his tablet. I see that this man has succeeded, first, in surprising Elsa and me and, secondly, to get us to listen to him attentively. When he looks at us, something in him instils confidence deep within me. I don't know how to describe it. Perhaps it is his white tunic or the way he moves his hands so deliberately, hands I've noticed, for the first time, are so large; hands of a man used to hard work, not writing or typing on a computer like I do. This man is special. However, as I look at him, I already know what he's going to say next.

"Yes, as you might have already guessed," says Nicola. "I am the watchman."

I think he was hoping to surprise us further with this last statement. In fact, Erik looks up from the map, gets up and walks to the window. Samuel seems to wink at me, with a half-smile. I hope he's not noticed anything on my face, not because I am not surprised, but because I don't know if this is all rubbish or something big.

"For the Romans, it was a sacred city and all of this because of this point on the map." He points at the intersection of the streets, "The balance of the four elements of nature, and this point would represent the fifth element – the ether. And throughout time, we've always monitored the direction of the wind. There has always been someone checking to see that the order of the cosmos is maintained. And it has always been maintained."

He stops suddenly as he focuses on the figurine of the head with the two faces under the window. He gets up slowly, picks it up in his hands, and then finishes his sentence:

"… Until now."

Erik's expression has changed. He now looks very interested. He can't take his eyes off the figurine with the two faces. Sofia is pensive as she observes him, and Elsa sits upright at the table to listen more closely. Undaunted by all that we have heard, Samuel continues drawing on his tablet.

Nicola stands up and walks to the window. Gazing at the weather vane, he continues talking:

"What has been happening for some time is that the wind at this point is no longer entering in the exact direction as it should. In other words, the *cierzo* is no longer entering directly through the Western Gate or going out by the Eastern. Moreover, although it cannot be seen from here, the Church of the Magdalena is no longer illuminated by the sun as it ought to be." He waits a second, and then continues: "... at least, as Rome had so ordained."

He gets us all to sit upright at the table and listen with all the attention that five 16-year-old boys and girls can give to something as if their lives depend on it.

"For this reason, all the force of the people living in Zaragoza, of the sun and the wind is getting weaker. The sacred city stops being sacred because the order of the Cosmos is not being maintained as it ought. And now... the people who have lived many years in Zaragoza are getting weaker, and are losing their balance and are literally falling over."

"Ah! So, it only affects adults who have been living here for many more years," Samuel concludes, without looking up from his tablet.

What a guy. He didn't seem to be paying attention.

After a moment of silence in the room, without looking at the rest of us and to the surprise of everyone, Elsa launches a question:

"And how can it be fixed?"

My first thought is that this girl has got too caught up in the story or else she is a little naive. The problem is that perhaps I am even more naive because I was going to ask the same question. But I didn't want to because I don't know what Sofia would think of me then. In any case, it is best to keep silent and wait for the answer.

"It cannot be fixed..." Nicola answers, looking at us mysteriously.

Wide-eyed, we all stir uncomfortably in our seats, Elsa with raised eyebrows, and I too. Samuel winks at me again. Erik turns his attention back to the old man's face. Sofia gets up suddenly from her chair to look out the window. The rest of us do the same. On the other side of the street, the weather vane has changed direction. At that moment, we hear Nicola saying:

"It cannot be fixed," followed by silence. Looking at the figurine below the window, he continues, "here."

Immediately Erik turns and asks:

"What do you mean by 'it cannot be fixed here'? Do you mean in this apartment? On this street? Or in this city?"

There is silence until Nicola, looking at each of us one by one, says:

"I say that it cannot be fixed... in this time. We have to go back in time to fix it."

CHAPTER 19

Thursday 22 December 2016.
Time: 1:05 pm

Sofia

The sun continues shining and the wind has not dropped in intensity. In winter in the Ebro Valley, you always need to have a coat, although the sun's rays make you think that it is warm. I can still remember my mother's response when I called her five minutes ago to say that I was not going home to eat. "Child, you've not come home to eat for several consecutive days." I didn't know what to tell her. I simply told her that it was for work with my classmates and said goodbye. I don't know if I am being a bad daughter, but this is beginning to engulf us and I want to be with my friends.

The entrance into the high school is next to the primary school, and depending on the time, we agree to meet up at the exit of the primary school while mums and dads wait for their children to take them home. Erik is leaning back against the wall with his leg bent at the knee to support his tablet.

While waiting for their children to come out, a small group of parents standing next to us talk among themselves with noticing that we are there.

One mother says to another, "I am very worried. On Sunday, my husband fainted at 4 o'clock in the afternoon, and could not get up on his feet. Since he has recovered, he has not been able to get up. Even I have had a problem with my ear that has forced me to stop doing a number of things because I feel that I am going to fall."

One of the fathers, pointing to the mobile in his hand, says:

"I believe that someone must do something. All the friends I have in the city have received the same message on their mobiles: '*Zaragoza collapses*'."

The third woman who had been listening crosses her arms and comments:

"My father says that it's a terrorist chemical attack causing some kind of illness that is affecting the tympanic membrane."

The other women, not only are they not laughing, but they gesticulate and shrug their shoulders. The father, who had been speaking about his mobile, again interrupts:

"My wife and I went on the web page <<zaragozacollapses.com>> and we were connected to a hyperlink which said: 'Zaragoza collapses and you know what to do'. We have no idea what it could be. Moreover, there is this strange sign with a crossed rectangle. No one knows what it means. I don't know if all of this is just a joke... but what is true is that we are all losing our balance. And that is real."

The first mother continues:

"I don't have any idea of what it means, but someone must do something..."

The mothers and fathers continue talking...

"Hello!" Someone says behind me.

Finally, Samuel arrives.

"Hi! How are you?" Elsa and I greet him simultaneously.

He has not changed his clothes. He has on the same long coat and pockets full as always. But something about him looks different. He looks strange today. As David comes up, I look at him again. Elsa watches me as she raises her hand to her head and turns to watch Samuel. I frown because I don't understand what she means. She does it again. He has combed his hair! It's true, he has combed his hair. It's the first time I've seen him like that. I smile at Elsa and give him the thumbs up with my right hand. She smiles back.

Samuel notices that we are all looking at him.

"Sorry I'm late."

My goodness. What's happening today? He is even apologising. I've never seen him do it before. Today must be a special day for him.

"Is it your birthday?" Elsa asks him.

We are obviously of the same mind.

But Samuel's expression clearly indicates that it isn't and that the question is all nonsense.

"How about doing something productive?" He says, looking down at his tablet.

I make a gesture for us to go and we leave so that we can talk without the adults listening.

We turn onto Goya Avenue heading for the centre and I almost bump into Elsa as we turn the corner. As I stand upright, supporting myself a little on her shoulder, I look straight ahead. Since they built the new urban train station under the avenue, this part of the city has taken on a futuristic look. The raised wooden roof with round shapes resembles the modern airports that they have built in recent years. I like it because, among so many old buildings, there is something new, which I am sure will not leave anyone indifferent.

The sunshine is not warm. The temperature has dropped and we cannot stop anymore. We continue walking without saying a word, and I use this opportunity to look at my friends.

Erik is exceptionally attractive today. He is wearing a close-fitting black jumper with a high collar, tight jeans and light brown boots. He is the only one who is not wearing a coat, so I imagine he is probably wearing three layers of clothes underneath. As we walk along the Gran Via Boulevard, he gives me his hand and I accept it. This time, it is I who decide to intertwine our fingers and it is not difficult because he allows me to do it so easily. We look at each other and I smile at him. I am enjoying it. When he took charge the other day at the Plaza de La Seo, he organised us to position the maps and drawings on the street. I felt so proud of him. He has not been in Spain for even a year and yet he already has a command of the language that he is able to make others follow him.

Walking abreast of each other and taking up the whole width of the street, we leave the cycle lane free and do not go across the gardens, but occupy almost the whole street. Despite the cold, there are also many people walking along the street, all hurrying along, fully protected with scarves and coats buttoned up to the neck. Avoiding us and without us getting in their way, they hurry along. If they only knew what is happening! Could it be any other way? Should we shout and tell them all about it? When there is a grave problem, shouldn't we all be aware of it? Or, is it better for others not to know so that they can remain happy? I don't know.

Regardless, today we know about it and we cannot be indifferent.

After not saying anything for a while, I feel that I should break the silence.

"We have to do something. I believe that it's only us and Nicola who know what is happening and what we have to do. Besides, tomorrow is 23rd December.

"But I think that this man is bonkers," Erik interrupts me, making me turn to look at him in the face as if to say 'let's see why you are contradicting me'. "What he said to us the other day, don't tell me if it isn't complete balderdash. I only see these things in cartoons on TV."

I release his hand.

"Perhaps it isn't such rubbish after all..." David begins and stops. I notice him looking at my hand.

On my right, I see Samuel give a small smile. David looks at Erik making a gesture you usually do when you are contradicting someone, without voicing the words aloud, but silently implying: 'sorry I've contradicted you, but I had to say it'. Then, he shrugs his shoulders but Erik is looking away. We stop at the corner of Gran Via Boulevard and Plaza Paraíso before going across the street at the pedestrian crossing towards Paseo Independencia. Without speaking we come closer to each other in a kind of circle.

It is full of people. Everyone in this city must be here, walking across this intersection. Because of this time of year, everyone is hurrying from one place to another, carrying bags from different shops and department stores. The Christmas lights, as in previous years, add a special touch to the centre. I

127

really like it. Those on the department stores on Paseo Sagasta have again amazed everyone with a spectacular design formed by thousands of coloured lights. It covers the whole facade of eight floors, featuring a reindeer with synchronised lighting which simulates the reindeer running.

Elsa looks from side to side, checking to see if there is anyone around to hear what she is about to say to us.

Then, she looks at each of us in turn:

"He said that we have to journey back in time to find the answer. He talked about jumping through a portal and about the music. That's all we have. All these people falling over do not have this information."

I turn around towards the direction from which we had come and on the last bench on the right opposite the Business Faculty, I can see two women who have lost their balance just as we were passing alongside. Fortunately, the third lady is okay and is attending to them.

It is not normal for five 16 year-olds to be talking about portals and travelling back in time. I feel stupid. If my little brother and sister had mentioned it at home, mum and I would be having a good laugh. If only it were so and it was *they* who were experiencing what we are going through now. I am sure that they would understand it better than I do. How can I believe in these kinds of things at my age? All the same, the problem is that the facts are the ones the old man talked about on the design of the city; and moreover, it's about the Romans.

"I have to confess something," Elsa cuts through my thoughts, "since the first day in class when they talked about the 'sacred city', I have been researching it." We all look at her without saying anything. "You know that I have been fascinated by History, but I have never told you that I absolutely love the Greek and Roman periods... but there is a link that has continued throughout the ages: geometry."

This girl is certainly a box of surprises!!! She's got my full attention. And the boys too, because the way she is describing it shows her command of the subject. The wind continues to blow hard. It is freezing and I really don't feel much like being in the street, and even less, in such an exposed spot. But none of us want to move. The daylight allows us to see the details of the grey close-fitting coat she is wearing. It looks very elegant on her.

"From what I read yesterday in a book by John Hirst, the true experts in geometry were the Greeks, apart from being the best philosophers of all time. When the Romans arrived, as experts in Engineering, it was more useful for them to fight and build an empire. But in everything else, they acknowledged that the Greeks were superior to them and they maintained what they had learnt from that culture..."

She is interrupted by the presence of a man who stops next to us. Elsa notices him and falls silent. While he stands there, she refrains from speaking. I don't know why he has stopped. Finally, he moves away and I turn back to continue listening to Elsa.

"... A member of the Roman elite knew how to speak Greek and Latin, the language of the Romans. They even sent their children to university in Greece or they would hire a Greek tutor to teach their children at home. In other words, all that we are seeing with regard to geometry in the city is basically from the Greeks. And it is the best way to see how intelligent they were. However, it is Sofia who could tell us more about the geometry..."

She looks at me and I nod as I make hand signals for her to continue giving her part of the story. I am not going to admit that I have no idea what she is talking about when she said that I am an expert on geometry.

"They saw geometry as a guide to the fundamental nature of the universe. One of the explanations for nature itself is that it is maintained by the balance of the four elements: water, earth, fire and air. It was one of the theories that gained most popularity among the Romans."

At that point, the man we had seen before came back. Erik notices him and motions to Elsa to stop. He overtakes us and crosses to the other side of the street. He seems to be waiting for someone because he does nothing else but look at his watch and cross from one side to another...

Elsa turns around to look at him and once she thinks that he is far enough, she continues:

"So, if the Romans wanted to build a sacred city, they needed to have exact geometrical forms and above all, to align them to the four elements of nature. At first, when they told us about it in class, it sounded like rubbish, but then I've been reading about it at home and I found out something that I did not expect."

She stops and looks at all of us. I felt Erik put his arm around my shoulders, but I almost take no notice as I am so engrossed in the story. All that Elsa is talking about and, particularly, the fact that she had verified it after class the other day seems so incredible. She has held out her hand for me to talk about the geometry, but I still cannot tell them what I know. Since we started this adventure, almost all the clues emerged while I was looking through the papers that my father had left back on his desk, the ones that my mother does not want to remove. Last night, I began to link geometry to the story that Nicola told us and I think that I found something. I cannot say yet because I want to confirm it again first.

Then, David interrupts her:

"I'd like to have more information before making a decision. I'm sorry, but I have to go home in a while because I promised my mother that I would lend a hand with something. Whatever you decide, I will agree with whatever the majority decides, even if it is to proceed with what Nicole said. Like you, I feel that this is all a madness, but what is happening in the city is even greater madness."

He turns and points at the women who have fainted on a bench on the street.

"I believe," David continues, "that we are the only people who know what is really happening, and we have a responsibility to make a decision. It's tomorrow and we're just in time. If you feel that we should meet up later today and continue..."

He does not get to complete his sentence when Erik surprises us all by speaking very loudly. If I weren't going out with him, I would have sworn that he is shouting at us.

"This is all rubbish! Let's be serious here. This man is mad and we are believing him?"

I take his hand off my shoulder and without looking at him, I say:

"Perhaps, it's not such rubbish!"

I have always been taught to be polite at all times, especially when there is conflict within a group. Here, I am making a great effort not to shout some obscenity at him. Calm down Sofia. Calm down.

Everyone else is looking at me, waiting for me to continue. I am not ready to say all that I had verified in recent days. I don't want them to think that I am mad, but I need more time to verify the information. So I will tell them some of what I have learnt.

"Since my father disappeared," I begin as I rummage around in my backpack, "my mother has been buying books on the history of Zaragoza. I don't know if this is a coincidence or not, but a few days ago, this book arrived at our home." I take out the book and I read the cover *Antiguas Puertas de Zaragoza* [Ancient Gates in Zaragoza] by Raquel Cuartero and Chusé Bolea."

I let them leaf through the book for a few seconds and then show them various chapters. The main aim of these authors was to describe the various gates in the city and show the role they each played throughout history. I remember that when my mother showed it to me, I began to read it immediately and finished it in one afternoon.

"Look! In this chapter, they talk about Valencia Gate, or the Eastern Gate, built by the Romans. In the excavations at the beginning of the last century, they found an ashlar with an inscription. Have a look."

As they approach the book, they can see a photo of what Valencia Gate looked like before it was destroyed, and you can clearly see the Church of la Magdalena behind the door itself. The photo would have been taken in the middle of the 20th century, and what I am showing them at this moment is the photo below. In this photo, you can see a piece of the Roman ashlar. It is a block of rectangular stone where one of the sides is divided vertically into two halves. The right half is not clear. Rather, there is a glimpse of something that was once engraved on it, but it is now destroyed. You can only just make out the relief of the marks which erased them. However, on the left side, there are five lines of written letters. Some of them are very clear, but in the third line, someone defaced it with marks to prevent it from being seen properly.

According to the authors, a possible interpretation of the letters and their translation into English:

PORTA ROMANA QUI FACIUN(T) TE LA(RES CE)DANT

"Roman Gate, let those who built you return to their country," I read aloud.

I look at their faces and everyone, except Erik, looks surprised.

"This ashlar," I continue, "is the one I was observing at the museum when the guide came and handed me this paper."

Samuel stands up and stares at me. Elsa and David look at me as if they had seen a ghost. Suddenly, Erik shouted angrily, with a strongly accented voice that he could not prevent:

"OK! Enough of this rubbish!"

CHAPTER 20

David

From the time I was small, my mother has been teaching us that in life we have to make decisions and it is very important to have all the information necessary to make the right decision, but as she would say: 'If you have to choose between waiting for years to have complete information, then perhaps it is best to make the decision with the information you have now'. I've always tried to follow this advice. But, at the same time, I prefer to have all the facts first before acting. With this issue, I want us to do the same, and to make a decision calmly. We cannot make a hasty decision. We have to take it easy.

Nicola amazed us the other day, by talking about the persistence of the people who live in this city. I understand it as the ability to keep progressing even if you fail or if something does not turn out right. Deep down... it is what I like, not only to make a decision but, specifically, to see the outcome. To make a decision, it's necessary to be prudent and to be certain before taking the first step. I like being practical... but with information.

It is precisely for this reason that I am beginning to feel uncomfortable. We have a lot of information to make a decision, but I am not sure if we have it all – what Nicola has told us, the maps, the history that Elsa was talking about and now what Sofia was able to find out about the stone from the Eastern Gate. It's obviously madness. But people are losing their balance and falling over, and they don't know why. We could spend hours, days or even years to get more information but, when do we stop and do something?

And now, here's this guy shouting that he is going. Well, let him! Although the person who really has to go is me because I will be in trouble with my mother if I don't get home at the time I said.

Elsa and I look at each other and don't quite know what to do. At the same time, Sofia is looking at Erik, but her face is a true reflection of dislike at this moment. She is flushed. Her expression changes to her characteristic narrowed eyes and pursed lips. From here, I can see how the skin on her face is moving like a sea of waves.

It's obvious that they are growing apart, although for me that's no bad thing. Erik looks around him, everywhere except at Sofia. He puts his hands in his trouser pockets and shrugs his shoulders. Our eyes met. He is not happy. He looks as if he is going to explode... but I don't feel sorry. Not one bit.

I look around to catch Samuel's eye and, typical, he is not looking at any of this. What a strange guy he is. In the middle of an argument between his companions, he is writing something – I don't know what – on the tablet he is carrying. The first day I saw him, I thought he was escaping into his device to play some rubbish game that freaks play. When I look at him a little while later, without him knowing, I see that he is writing with one of those applications with which you write on the screen with your finger and then it types it up for you. As I watch him, I say to myself that it really doesn't matter what he's doing. But the truth is, after what happened in the ice cream parlour, I am curious to know all that he does, especially at this moment, which is the first time we have had a similar commotion since.

"It's incredible," Elsa says, trying to calm the situation. "It is difficult to believe it, but it's totally in line with the portal Nicola told us about. I don't know who wrote it or why they did, but certainly the coincidence is impressive: a gate to travel back to Rome." She makes inverted comma signs on the word. "To travel... back in time." She repeats the inverted comma signs.

Erik steps back from the group. This is getting more interesting by the moment. I don't know what has annoyed him

134

more, Sofia taking his arm off her shoulder or the fact that she's contradicting him. Well, these things happen. I avoid his gaze to prevent him from seeing what I feel inside. He is seriously angry. I have never seen him like this.

"I think that you are all bonkers!!!" He shouts angrily, looking at everyone else but Sofia. "This is all unreal and I am not prepared to go on with this farce. I'm going home. Do what you want."

I can't believe it! Sofia's face is a picture. She is absolutely stunned by the force of his reaction. It is completely out of character. He was probably waiting for Elsa to finish or not to say anything and afterwards to tell Sofia alone, on her own, that he didn't want to continue with this business. However, he chose to have a scene. It does not make sense. I cannot say anything. Elsa and I look at each other. What a mess. Each one of us staring at something or other, not knowing quite what to say.

Finally, Elsa breaks the silence.

"But you can't go." She falls silent for a moment, "Nicola said that the jump has to be on the 23rd, at dawn tomorrow."

A gust of wind made us all turn away and we stopped looking at each other for a moment.

"We should drop all this nonsense," Erik demands in louder voice.

We look at him. He turns around and walks away along Paseo Pamplona towards Carmen Gate. At no point, did he address Sofia. She can't take her eyes off him, but I can't say that I am not pleased by what has just happened.

There is silence as Erik walks away.

"Well go!" Sofia shouts after him without Erik hearing, since he is lost among the crowd crossing at the lights.

We all look at her, even Samuel who looks up from his tablet for a moment. It is the first time that I see him open his eyes wide and raise his eyebrows. What must he be thinking?

The two women passing, dressed in expensive fur coats, observe the scene and with disgust, turn away. The man who we had seen approaching us before, stops. He turns his gaze in the direction Erik has just gone and sets off also towards Carmen Gate. How strange!

I watch Elsa looking around to decide on what next to do. I don't believe what I am seeing. However, I hope that she does not see the slight smile on my face when Erik walks away.

"Do you know who that man is?" Elsa's question startles me.

She is gazing in the distance towards where Erik has gone. As she gets no response from anyone, she turns and adds:

"While we were standing here and talking, it appeared that he was listening to us, almost spying. When he moved away on the two occasions, I didn't place any importance on it." She falls silent for a moment. "Now that I see him following Erik, when he turned around towards us this last time, I recognised him..."

Just then, a group of boys rush past us, pushing us aside, trying their best to get to the stop in order not to miss the next tram. I have to hold on to Elsa for her not to fall over. We watch them running to get onto the coach.

We turn back towards her. She must have felt our eyes on her:

"He was the guard at the museum, the one who grabbed my hand when I was leaving."

Hang on! This is getting serious!

I glance around and see that Samuel has turned back to his tablet, although this time I see a mischievous smile on his face. I can't understand anything.

"What must he be thinking if he treats us like idiots?" Sofia ignores what Elsa has said and continues to look in the direction her boyfriend has gone.

I notice that Elsa is trying to say something, I imagine, to lighten the tension.

"And now, what do we do?"

Well, an intervention. No one seems surprised that they are following us. In the end, is the woman in the ice cream shop right, and this is dangerous?

Sofia is still angry. She turns around to face us and, unexpectedly, it serves to calm her down. She looks at me, at Elsa and then at Samuel. He looks up from his screen and returns her gaze. I see how her expression changes. Inside, she must be dying of shame for shouting in the middle of the street, as super-polite as she is normally. She was flushed.

After a brief silence, Sofia announces, looking down on the ground:

"For now, I'm going home." She heads off back along the Gran Via Boulevard, and then towards Goya Avenue.

"I'm off too," says Samuel, and he goes in the opposite direction along Paseo Independencia.

This guy is unpredictable. I don't know if I'll ever understand anything he does.

As I look at Elsa, I see that she is as disappointed as I am. We are almost the same height. But today, she is wearing heels and so I have to look up at her. I've known her for years, but it's the first time I've been alone with her. I know that she has two brothers. I know where her parents are from, but I don't know anything more about her. Actually, there are many more people in our class for whom I could say the same – to be in the same school or area for so many years and yet know nothing about them, other than the basic information. In our case, it's nonsense because we've been together in the same class from the beginning of the school year. Now that I think of it, we get on very well, but we've never spoken about anything other than our studies.

Today, I have discovered something about her that I had not seen before. She tried to bring calm to the two episodes of conflict in which we tried not to take sides and to propose alternatives. I do remember one thing. There was a time in class last year when something similar had happened and she tried to make peace in a way that was so delicate, but effective all the same. She has a way about her that is modest, which comes in handy when these conflicts occur.

I must have been staring at her for a long time because she looks away from me.

"Sorry Elsa," I start apologising, "for staring at you." Then, I lie to her, "I was trying to remember what you were saying before and when you stopped, you were going to say something that was important for you."

I can see that she has become relaxed once more and is smiling.

"You said that you were in a hurry. You had to go out with your mother," she replies. I feel a little confused. "I'll walk along with you. I have to go the same way anyway," she continues and I feel more comfortable.

We head for the top of Paseo Sagasta without speaking as she knows that I live in Torrero.

It is difficult to walk and talk on a windy day like this in this city because you can hardly hear yourself speak. But when she speaks, she does it so clearly and with so much passion, it reduces problems in hearing. This girl continues to impress me, not only for what she knows, but also for the way she tells it.

Besides, she looks exceptionally pretty today.

As we walk together, she continues, "What I was going to say earlier is linked to something that I have noticed: that what the teacher explained in class and what Nicola mentioned have something in common. And it has something to do with balance."

She stops speaking because, just at that moment, the woman walking past us stops in her tracks and appears as if she wanted to listen to us. I watch her face. I've seen her before, but I can't remember where. She realises that I am looking at her, but does not move away. As there are so many people in the street, she looks like any other person.

I make a sign to Elsa for us to stop in front of the shop window of the shop on our right. She is surprised and frowns. I raise my eyebrows and I open my eyes wide to let her know that the woman is trying to listen. She smiles and nods, and motions me with her head to look to my right.

As I do as she suggests, I understand what she's getting at. Looking at a woman's lingerie shop to throw off a nosy woman is perhaps not the best choice. I also smile. As the woman walks away, Elsa takes my arm and we continue walking in this strong freezing wind. Anyone seeing us would think that we are boyfriend and girlfriend. But I can only think of Sofia.

"This is all amazing!" As if nothing had happened, Elsa continues chatting as we walk along the pavement. "Because, apart from my love for history, I am free. Although it may be nonsense, I have always felt that I have been searching for this balance. For a few consecutive days I've been hearing the same thing, and when I analyse the history of the city, I can only say that I agree with Nicola, that it is all falling apart."

She stops again because at the lights, where we are going to cross, there are lots of people, and between us, we are creating an air of mystery which, it appears, we need to hide from everyone.

Once we are on the other side of the street, with the Ebro Hydrographic Confederation building on our right and with no one near us, Elsa continues talking. It's fascinating when someone tells you something with so much passion.

"One of the most important themes in the history of the city which has aroused a lot of interest is the ability of different religions and cultures to live side by side in peace for so many years and after so many wars and invasions. It has always surprised me: this balance, let's say, between Christians, Muslims and Jews."

How interesting. Just a few days ago, we were talking about that at home. This is the opposite of *Oh Jerusalem*, a film we saw with my mother a couple of weeks ago. It is the opposite of balance. From ancient times, different regions have been in dispute. I recognise that I don't understand it very well, but there is always something about that on the radio or on TV.

"When Nicola talked about balance the other day," Elsa continues. "he linked it to the Romans. I was at home, reading about the era in which the city was founded in the book by John Hirst, the one I told you about the other day."

She takes out the book from her backpack as she's walking, and shows me the cover.

"As they have already told us, it was Emperor Augustus who did it. And I found out information I didn't know."

She stops just next to the bank on the street where we're standing. She sits and motions me to sit down next to her.

"When Brutus assassinated Julius Caesar to prevent one man from governing the Republic, there was a civil war. In all this mess, a victorious man appeared. He was the grand-nephew of Julius Caesar who adopted him as his son. In 27 B.C., he was proclaimed the first Roman Emperor."

She is quiet for a moment. She looks at me with a mischievous smile hovering on her face.

"He was a very astute man. He maintained republican institutions."

Her expression makes me laugh. It is a mixture of seriousness and a complicitous smile. Now she is going to tell me something which for her must be the clue to all this confusion.

"In fact, he did not want to be called *Emperor*, but simply *First Citizen*. Augustus viewed his work as being a kind of facilitator, or so he wanted others to think, that he alone would help the machinery to work smoothly."

At any other time, this wouldn't have interested me, but as they celebrated the 2000th anniversary of the death of the Emperor Augustus in the city two years ago, we had to study him in class. A few interesting things remained with me, but I have to acknowledge that I had not heard this part of the story before.

"What impressed me most about this man is..."

Suddenly, my mobile rang. I search for it in my coat pocket and take it out. Elsa stops speaking and waits. I look at the screen. It's the telephone number of my house. Oh gosh. My mother's going to give me a hard time! I show her the screen, and looking at her with raised shoulders, I indicate that I have to go home soon.

"Hi mum. I'm going home now." I speak first as I answer the phone.

But then, my expression changes so much that Elsa looks worried. I only listen. I can't believe what I am hearing. Feeling a mixture of impotence, agitation and dread, I end the call. Elsa stares at me. I look at her as I've never looked at anyone before. With my eyes fixed on hers, I explain:

"It's my little brother. My mother has just fainted at home."

CHAPTER 21

Thursday 22 December 2016
Time: 2:30 pm

Sofia

"Is that you, dear?"

I hear my mother's voice from the kitchen as I close the front door behind me. As always, I drop my keys in the first drawer of the hall table next to the entrance into the apartment.

"Yes, mum. It's me. I've just arrived," I respond.

"That's early! I expected you later." I hear her saying from a distance.

There is no other sound in the flat.

I look in the mirror at the entrance.

I watch my reflection in the mirror as I think about what has just happened in the last half an hour. After leaving my companions, I walked home quickly. I had never felt like this before. I had never walked so quickly or felt so angry. I didn't look at anyone.

When I walk, I normally like observing other people's faces. I also like looking up towards the sky. Sometime ago, a friend told me that people who live in this city tend to walk hunched over, looking down at the ground. I told him that it was really because of the strong wind in the city, as a joke, but I understood what he was getting at. I then began to focus on the way people were walking and realised that many people only look down at the ground and, therefore, very few look up to the tops of the trees or the buildings. Only tourists do that, I thought, when he said it. So, since then, I have tried not to miss the slightest detail, but instead to look and observe everything around me.

I even succeeded in discovering very interesting details in the buildings.

My most recent discovery was the weather vane that Nicola told us about.

I have often walked down Don Jaime Street, but it is only since meeting this man that I have looked up and seen the weather vane turn according to the wind. It is certainly mysterious after all that I have heard.

But today, I have broken my personal promise and did not look at anyone.

I came directly home.

I remained standing outside our front door for several minutes before opening it. I didn't know what to say to my mother to explain why I've come home so early. In recent days, I had convinced her that I would getting back later for the rest of the week because of the History project I am doing with my mates. But I have come back without having an excuse prepared.

I felt the silence again.

Fortunately, she hasn't come to ask me anything. It's best because I won't have to lie to her.

I look in the mirror, from my head down.

I've changed. It's been a while since I've looked at myself so closely. I'm no longer a child. I've even changed in the way I behave. My parents have brought me up strictly. I've always had to follow rules and schedules. I believe that at home, no one has ever broken a rule. They've also taught us to behave ourselves, to be mindful of good manners, ways of behaving, words and speaking little. "If you don't have anything to say, then it's best to be quiet", my father would always say. "And if you do, then do it nicely," he would finish after a silence.

It's an elegance which seemed almost excessive in being polite. I am aware that my friends make fun of how I say things, and I don't like that. The truth is that I want to show them who I really am. I want to change, or perhaps I want others to change. Oh, I don't know.

The problem is that everything around me is changing too fast and I don't know if I'm prepared for it. I like making quick decisions and getting on with it, but now, with all that Nicola has said, I feel we don't have sufficient information.

I lower my gaze. I feel cold, suddenly frozen.

Hey! What's this?

What I'm seeing has struck me like a dagger in my chest. It's something that had already become a custom at home, but I didn't question the reason for it.

Under the mirror, my parents had put a small chest of drawers and on it some small ornaments. There has always been one there. It was a welcome greeting that they were given when they got married. It was painted on ceramic in a village nearby and stuck onto a small wooden plinth so that it could be placed upright and be seen when you enter. Two days before disappearing, my father brought home a ceramic representation of the *yin yang* on two ceramic plates, one white and the other black, in a semi-circular shape, concave at one end and convex at the other, so that when one penetrates the other, the two form a single circle.

Until today, I had not paid much attention to it since that first day. Now as I recall it, when he put it there, his only words were, "This will be our symbol of balance." And for the last few days, I've heard nothing else but that word in the city.

I can't stop looking at the ornament. Something is going through my mind, something very strange. I don't feel well. I am getting dizzy. I lean against the chest and look again at the *yin yang*. I become steady once more and hurry to my father's old office. I rush in. My mind is racing a mile a minute. I can't feel my legs, but I am moving them as fast as I can. I switch on the light and turn to my right without looking. I almost stumble over his briefcase he left on the floor against the wall.

I go directly to his desk and stop. There it is.

Every time I come in here, I can't stop looking at it. It's as if I had created a nostalgic shrine of refuge to my dad in the photo I am holding in my hands. The problem is that the same thing always happens. I can't prevent it.

144

I dry my tears with my left hand, but I can't stop looking at it.

It's a photo I like a lot, but since he is not here, it has become almost necessary to look at it. Here he looks happy, without wearing a suit and tie, as I like to see him, to go and give classes at the university. Here, he looks as if he's just come out of an *Indiana Jones* film, dressed in the same beige colour, in trousers, shirt and bomber jacket. You could say that he is somewhat more modern than the character in the movie because the boots are more typical of those used for present day trekking in the mountains and he never wore a hat. Instead, he preferred to wear a red kerchief tied around his head in a way that left some material hanging down behind him to protect the back of his neck from the sun. What made him look most peculiar were the sunglasses he always wore. They were those round types with leather protective strips on the sides like those worn to go up the Himalayas. The trouble is that for me he was *Indi*. My dad was Indiana Jones for me.

I've to dry my tears again. Many memories flood into my mind.

How good it is to see someone doing something that makes him happy! He also liked teaching in the city, but in this photo he was radiant. He was happy. In this photo, he looks it, especially as he was arm-in-arm with my mum, giving a show of unity in the team they were. She looked particularly pretty in the photo.

To anyone looking at her, my mother is a person of average height, with skin bronzed by the sun and with an athletic look. She's always told us that her work as an archaeologist required her to go on long treks to distant places, and sometimes when she was busier than normal with a find, she would hardly eat and would even have to sleep outdoors wherever she was.

Even last year, we three children would spend long periods of time listening to Dad and Mum relating their adventures. They were a perfect couple, albeit a little unusual. Dad was a typical university historian, already balding and always wearing his little round glasses. Because of his appearance, you would never imagine the places he managed to get to. Fortunately, I had this photo to see the other side of the coin. My mum, a field archaeologist, constantly had field trips (as she called it) that would take her one or two weeks away from home. They were only able to go together on very few occasions. The one in the photo was their last.

To date, it's been a year since they had gone on a field trip, just around the time my father left us.

Oh! I almost dropped the photo. I've begun to be distracted.

"What's that?"

There's something that I had never noticed before in the lower left corner.

Of course, because I always put my thumb here I could not see it. It's strange because, although I can't see it clearly, it looks familiar. In the photo, Dad has his left arm on my mum's shoulders. What I could never see was that he is holding something in his right hand which is hanging down at his side. He is holding it in his fist, but a part of it is sticking out at the top. It's a very small statue and only its head can be seen. My goodness!

I want to be sure. Where does he have it?

I search through the papers on the desk. Everything is disorderly as when he was here. There are papers everywhere.

Here it is. I've got it!

I look at the photo as closely as I can and with my father's magnifying glass I try to make out what he has in his hand. Yes, that is it. It's a little figure with a head with two faces like the one we saw at the entrance of Nicola's house. I can't believe it!

I feel my heart pounding and my breathing quickening. All the information we've been gathering these days is all around me. Everything is here, but I can't see the connections. How is all this possible? I don't believe in coincidences.

I turn quickly and pick up my father's briefcase that my mom has never wanted to move from here.

146

It is in dark brown leather and looks quite worn because he took it everywhere. Whenever I enter this room, I've always known it was there but, until this moment, I've never touched it. I am sure that mum will be annoyed, but I'm not worried. It's all accelerating by the minute and I can't stop.

Carefully, I place it on the desk on all the books and disorganised documents. Slowly, one by one, I take out the papers and photos he has in the only place to keep things. Inside, it is clean and well-ordered. Nothing like the top of his desk.

What I see leaves me stunned and I prefer to sit down.

I throw myself onto the chair and... ay! I'm falling. I'm falling. I cannot told on to anything.

Ow!

What a blow! What a stupid chair! I lost my balance, hardly making any movement. I've fallen with the chair landing on top of me. Damn! I've shattered the silence in the apartment.

I move the chair away, but remain sitting on the floor. I stretch out my legs and hold on to the briefcase. What impressed me before is now resting on my legs.

There are two books, a sheet with a series of numbers and two photos. As I put them together, I check each item.

The books are the original texts in English. There is a book titled *Sacred Geometry*, by one Robert Lawlor, and another smaller book which seems to be about the same thing, titled *Golden Section*, and according to my translation of the cover, it refers to the 'Greatest secret in Nature'. The author is one Scott Olsen. There is a loose white sheet of paper with a succession of numbers written on it, which I don't understand.

0, 1, 1, 2, 3, 5, 8, 13, 21, 34, 55...

But what impressed me most are the photos. In one I can see the little figure with the head with two faces. It must be what Dad is holding in his hand in the photo on the desk.

And the other...

It can't be!

It gave me a knot in my throat. It is the photo of the ashlar discovered at the Eastern Gate in the city of Zaragoza. Including this picture, I have seen it three times in less than a week.

My mind is really racing back to each occasion in recent days, recalling each moment when I saw these two images, but I can't find a connection. I get up.

"Are you OK, Sofia?"

I see my mother standing in the doorway, anxious after running, which she must have done when she heard the noise I made.

I nodded to say yes, knowing that I'm not going to like what is coming, judging from her expression at seeing the disorder I have caused.

"What are you doing here?" Her voice has taken on an aggressive tone as she looks angrily at me.

I have very seldom seen her like this, but when she is, it's best not to go near her.

At this moment, this average height lady lost all the sweetness she had during this last year. She is really angry, but I don't understand because, since my father's death, she's never forbidden us from entering this room. The only other thing I've done was simply to open his briefcase.

"Darn it, Mum! I fell and all you can do is to have a go at me!"

This leads to an uneasy silence between us, a silence you could cut with a knife. I can hardly believe what I said to her. Not only is it the first time I've sworn at home, but it is also the first time that I have answered her back.

I am going to try to lighten the situation.

"I wanted to see the photo on the table again and..." As I answer her, I realise that it's not going to be enough for her to calm down. "And I fell, Mum!" I end up shouting.

She violently snatches the books, photos and sheet of paper from my hands. She says nothing and returns them to the briefcase. As if she knew from memory where everything was,

148

she returns them in exactly the same place where they were when I fell. I can't take my eyes off her, because I don't understand anything that's happening.

I stand in front of her. We are now the same height, but her authority is not determined by height.

"Never in your life have you treated me worse that you have just done! If your father were here..." At that moment, she stops suddenly and looks behind me in the direction of his desk. "Now, get out, and I don't want you to be in here today," she says and without looking at me, she pushes me towards the door of the room.

As I leave, I look back trying to find answers by looking around, and there it was in the distance: the sign of the rectangle with crossed lines on a larger circle. But it was not on the table. I don't know if my heart could stand so many emotions in one day. It's the small poster hanging on the wall opposite the desk. It can't be. I've never noticed it before. It was right under my nose the whole time.

My father was working less than a metre away from the sign that the guide had given me on a crumpled piece of paper at the museum, the same sign that I had seen on the new webpage, the same sign Nicola had everywhere in his house.

When we are both outside the room, I turn to my mother and ask her:

"What was Daddy working on before he died?"

For the rest of my life, I don't think that I'll ever forget the expression on my mother's face. Her whole face, her bony cheekbones, her green eyes and beautiful smile showing those teeth, brilliantly cared for ever since childhood, undergo a transformation. At first, I thought that it was anger and fury, but looking at her closely, I realise that it was fear.

She does not look away either. I begin to feel very uncomfortable. I don't know what to say. She must have realised that I am beginning to get frightened and she quickly makes an effort to control her emotions.

She turns away from me, closes the door and, without meeting my gaze, she moves away and says:

"As of today, you are forbidden from entering this room."

CHAPTER 22

Thursday 22 December 2016
Time: 3:00 pm

David

"I've already told you that we would be arriving in 15 minutes..."

The words of the taxi driver rouse me from my thoughts as he takes me home.

"...It's always the same. Fifteen minutes. The traffic lights on this route are well-synchronised and there are normally no problems. If there are works or a traffic jam, they immediately make an alternative route available. So it's always 15 minutes from the place I pick you up to the area where you live."

I wasn't listening to him at first, but what he said just now made me remember what we've been talking about these days with regard to the city - the famous balance. Would Emperor Augustus be aware of what he had achieved? A city that is continually modifying itself or adapting to re-establish balance if something has been altered. 'A city in constant search for balance', the city's promotional slogan, comes to mind. "Why has this never occurred to anyone else before?" This was the last thing Elsa said to me. It left me intrigued because she wasn't able to finish the story as a result of my brother's call.

"But lately, we have to recognise that there are more traffic jams..." The taxi driver commented again.

When I said goodbye to Elsa, I checked to see if I had some money with me, and without a second thought, I stretched out my hand in the street to stop a taxi. I wanted to reach home as soon as possible. I believe that he must have felt sorry for me. Because of how nervous I was when I got into his taxi, he's not stopped speaking in order to help me calm down.

"...People have been fainting in their cars. Fortunately, until now, it's happened mainly when they were standing at the

151

traffic lights. The problem is that it's causing quite a lot of alarm in case it happens while they are driving." The taxi driver concluded just as we stopped in front of my building.

I am afraid. I don't know what I'm going to find at home. My mother unable to regain her balance just like the other people collapsing in the city? Until now, I thought that it could only happen to others, but not to any of the five of us.

I get out of the taxi and run to the front door. I can't find my keys. I put them in the outer pocket of my backpack, but they are not there. Or perhaps I put them inside? I don't know. I can't remember. I am beginning to get nervous because they're not inside either. I look inside the hall to see if a neighbour has come down and can open the door for me. No one is there. Finally, without thinking about it, I put my hand in my trousers' pocket and feel the bunch of keys which I had put into my pocket when I rushed out of the apartment this morning. I manage to open the door. Just at that moment, one of the neighbours comes out of the lift and greets me. There's no time to return the greeting because I immediately run up the stairs. It's only three floors, but I wouldn't know what to do, alone in the lift in the time it takes to arrive at our floor. I'd go crazy and I prefer to avoid that.

Marco has already put our mother on her bed. He's calm. He tells me what has happened.

Apparently, she had fainted while she was working at the computer in her office. My brother was studying in his room when he heard the thud. He called her, but she didn't answer. So he got up and went to find her. He found her with her head on the computer. He saw that she had a cut on her forehead and that it was bleeding. Carefully, he picked her up and put her on her bed. Then, he went for the medical kit, and with a sterile gauze and some hydrogen peroxide, he cleaned the wound. Afterwards, he called me.

This room has always given me a feeling of loneliness. Since our father's death, I remember that this room has always been tidy: the bed perfectly made with this pink bedspread with white flowers; the white wooden bedside table with a small lamp on top for reading; the alarm clock and a pile of books on the only shelf below. The white colour of the walls is only interrupted by the window, with the mirror above the dressing table for applying make-up and the large picture on the wall behind the bed. My mother likes the sea, as do my brother and I. A couple of years ago, we gave her this beautiful sunset over the Pacific so that the sadness she felt in this room would disappear because, here, she was filled with loneliness and nostalgia.

When our father died, she changed her room for this smaller one and gave us the large one. The apartment has only two bedrooms. Although I like it, I don't normally like talking about it with my friends because I think they live in larger homes. My mother spends much of her time here. She hardly ever goes to the living room. Her route around the house goes from the kitchen, our room, the bathroom and then back to her room. I don't know why she doesn't like sitting in the armchair, at least to watch a film with us. It's difficult to get into the mind of someone, especially hers.

The dressing table is at the foot of the bed. It's a small table, also in white, full of cosmetics. It's perhaps the only corner of the room where there isn't a lot of order because my mum spends a lot of time sitting there. She's always well made-up, even within the house. Sometimes, I think that she is obsessive, although I have to admit that she does it with elegance and class, but I've never said that to her.

Next to the dressing table and the window is the area she calls her office, which is nothing more than a table, a chair and a three-drawer cabinet on casters. I can imagine her bent over with her head on the laptop she uses, with her body illuminated by the bright sunlight entering through the curtainless window, the scene that would have confronted Marco.

Now she is on the bed.

I don't know if any boy of 14 would have reacted as my brother did. What I do know is that we two boys have been brought up alone with my mother. From what I can see in the rest of my class mates, when one of their parents has suddenly gone and the other has to take charge of everything, life takes a different turn for the children. It's difficult to explain why. I've seen many cases among people I know when you try to see how they get on with other young people of your own age. In our case, someone might say that we've become somewhat cold and hard. Often, it's difficult to interact with others in a group when we prefer to do things on our own. It's not that we're poorly behaved. It is just that we are accustomed to making decisions for ourselves. This would have made my brother react quickly because if my mother had remained in the position she was in for a long time, the wound might have developed complications and she could even have drowned by losing consciousness as a result of the blow.

Since the cases of people fainting started, the Town Hall has organised a support service for people suffering this problem in the street and there is also a consultation service for all family and friends who have to help someone. Our mother talked about it with us only last night and explained the advice that was given if it occurred within the home. The first was to check to see if the person who lost his balance is injured and to deal with it immediately, then move him, make the area safe and finally put him to bed. The support services also request that they be informed by telephone of how it happened, with name and surnames so that the details of sufferers could be entered into a register. They have to know how many people there are to be 'cured' when a way is found to do so, and no one can be excluded from the actions to be carried out.

"And now, what do we do?" He asks as he looks at me.

He had already called the Town Hall service to include our mother's name in the register. It is here that I feel the responsibility of being the older brother. We are accustomed to making decisions, after weighing up all the alternatives with time, but this is different. When we had questions about anything, we would seek the advice of our mother, and

154

although she did not tell us what to do, she showed us another option that we had not yet considered. Then, she left us to make our own decision. But today, she is not conscious to help us to make the next move.

"She already told us that if this happened," I replied seriously and firmly at the same time. "We would have to call Uncle Daniel and go with him."

Uncle Daniel is the only brother of my mother. He also lives in the city, and the truth is that we got on very well with our three cousins. I know that just the thought of calling my uncle will please Marco. He's a very purposeful man. I am sure that he will help us.

Precisely for this reason, when I call him to explain what had happened, I am not surprised he responded immediately, without complaint, and tried to be optimistic.

"Don't worry about anything, David," he tells me on the telephone. "I am coming to meet the three of you now and you will stay with us until this is all resolved."

"Thanks, Uncle. Thank you very much," I answer. "Please take my mum and my brother. I have something very important to do."

At that moment, I hear a signal on my mobile indicating I have a new message. I read it while I am still on the line to my uncle. "Meet me in half an hour at the Church of La Magdalena." Sofia has sent it.

CHAPTER 23

Thursday 22 December 2016
Time: 4:00 pm

Sofia

Since my father's disappearance a year ago, it's the first time that I've felt so bad. Fortunately, I'm surrounded by people and I walk unnoticed. Today, I need to feel as one of a crowd, to hide among the multitude. The city is big enough to be able to go out and not have to meet people you know at every corner, of course on streets where I assume that my acquaintances will not be present.

The incident with my mother just now has left me confused, frightened and very angry at the same time. Although I think it's worse for her as, after she closed the door of my father's office and forbad me from entering, I grabbed my coat, my bag, my mobile and left the house without a word. I know that it's not the right thing to do, but what she did was awful and I have to make my protest felt in some way.

I'm already beginning to feel better. I don't know if that's because it's been a while since, or if it is because I'm looking up at the famous metallic weather vane Nicola showed us.

It's there still. It's special. I observe the people passing under it, and no one looks up at it. The wind continues blowing from the northwest and the weather vane continues to point in the opposite direction. Gradually, I shift my gaze towards the window where Nicola lives, but I can only see the same white curtain drawn as always, without seeing anything inside. I am sure that none of the people milling around here know what we know: that the balance has been broken and therefore people are collapsing in the street; and that, according to this man, who we barely know but have come to respect, we have to travel back to the past to discover the balance that has been broken and try to re-establish it. I suppose that, if at this moment I said this to anyone passing by me, they would think I was mad and not take any notice of me.

I am at the margin of incredulity, irrationality and need to do something urgently. There are only a few more hours to the time he mentioned when we have to make the 'jump' and we don't yet have the clue that he told us we needed to find, and he could not help us in this. He only told us that for the first 'jump', the portal only opens once a year at dawn of the winter solstice, just when the light shines directly on the intersection between Don Jaime Street and Calle Mayor.

And I am standing here, at the very same spot, right now.

It still seems mad. According to the old man, in this same place, only something totally unreal can be opened. But what else can we do? The city continues to lose its balance and the authorities do not know what to do. It's in the news and since this morning the city is full of TV news channels from other countries and a load of journalists talking in different languages. 'The sacred city... the capital of balance' are the only things that come to mind.

However much I turn, I have come to a decision: we have to follow the advice Nicola had given us. So I set off to walk along Calle Mayor to the Church of La Magdalena.

My mobile is ringing. I look at the screen and I am dumbfounded when I see that it is Erik calling.

"Hello," I answer listlessly, after it rang five times.

"We have to talk! We have to talk!" He surprises me, speaking very quickly, with a highly agitated tone of voice. I expected first an apology for his behaviour earlier. "Sofia, I need to tell you something very important."

I hesitate for a moment because I've had so many emotions today. I don't know if this is all a dream or if it is reality. I relax, but I do not stop walking to where I am going.

"I'm meeting up with David, Samuel and Elsa at the Church of La Magdalena. You can come if you wish."

"No, no." He replies again in an agitated voice. He calms down a little before continuing. "Everything that's happening to us may have an explanation and I have just found out something that I have to tell you. But, I can only tell you."

Now I don't know what to think. The boy with whom I am going out makes a fuss, goes off in a huff when we are all together, does not call for several hours afterwards and when he does, tries to add urgency with a mystery.

"Look Erik," I respond, a little annoyed. "I don't know what you want to tell me, but I think you ought to come. Samuel, David, Elsa and I are continuing with this because it's all begun to take on a greater dimension."

"But..." Erik cuts in.

"Come," I interrupt without letting him finish, "or make an appointment online." I end the call.

What could he be thinking?! How could he think that he can behave so badly and pretend that nothing has happened?

The hoot of a car horn brings me back to the present. I realize that I have been walking while talking on the mobile and was about to cross the St Vincent de Paul Street without looking, with the pedestrian light on red. I almost dropped the mobile on the ground. Fortunately I caught it. If not, the car would have smashed it to pieces. What would I do without my mobile?

After crossing the street, I continue on my way and notice how narrow the street is, particularly in the last section on the left where the side wall of the church is located. It's a very interesting area because when I pass here, I see a great mixture of cultures, people of many races and religions passing next to one of the places which, as we now know, was crucial to the design of the city.

And here it is! I am now in the Plaza de la Magdalena.

It's the first time I have come here since we began hearing about the solstice rectangle, since Nicola told us the story. It continues to hold a mystery as always and, perhaps, even more so for me. But before looking at the plaza, I turn my head to the right. Even more carefully than ever before, I again observe the painting of what the Eastern Gate looked like years ago when it

158

still existed, on the wall of the building. I stop. I watch the archway of the gate and behind it, you can see the entrance of the church. It is strange that, in the photos and pictures of this church, which I have seen recently, the entrance catches the sun. You can see people from previous eras walking by and...

"Oh! Goodness gracious!" It's the only thing I can say. I can't move. "I can't believe it!"

A woman walking by stopped! I feel her at my side, also looking up. She must have heard me.

Standing in front of the great mural, there in the painting on the wall on the right, I see the same inscription on the ashlar at the museum and, subsequently, in the photo in my father's briefcase.

The woman continues on her way not before looking at me and shaking her head from right to left. I don't know what expression was painted on my face.

When I turn, I see David and Elsa sitting on one of the benches in the plaza. But something is wrong. David is pale. He looks very sad. Elsa seems to consoling him.

CHAPTER 24

Thursday 22 December 2016
Time: 4:30 pm

David

"Are you looking at the same thing that I am looking at?" Elsa, sitting next to me, startled me.

The two of us arrive five minutes before Sofia, and although we see her standing looking at the painting opposite, Elsa continues to converse with me to cheer me up.

"The Church of La Magdalena," she begins to tell me, "One of the buildings which impress me most in this city. According to what we had to study for the last exam in History last year, it is in the Mudéjar style of the 14th century, although it appears to have been described as a Romanesque church in 1126. Later, the interior was renovated in the 17th and 18th centuries in the Baroque style. The original structure and the square brick tower were maintained. From what I know, I think that it is one of the prettiest church towers, especially at night when it is lit up."

I am thankful for the distraction. All that has happened has made me very nervous.

"The truth," I answer her, so as not to be discourteous, "is that, from all that we have seen in class last year and analysing it from the perspective of recent days, Mudéjar art has something to do with..."

"Balance!" Elsa interrupts me like a little girl who could read my thoughts and enjoy showing it off.

"Well yes. That is what I was thinking." I look at her and smile because she's succeeded. I continue, "In fact, it is because of co-existence in mediaeval Spain and the result of mixing Christian and Muslim artistic expressions of the period."

I stand up. Her large eyes continue to hold me in their gaze. When she smiles, her white teeth contrast with her dark complexion and makes her face even prettier.

"You knew it well!" I continue, smiling, almost back to my normal self. "I was already aware last year that you liked that period of history."

She shrugs her shoulders. I notice that she is blushing. I stop looking at her.

Sofia is already here. At last, she's approaching the bench where we're waiting for her. The two of us are sitting on the backrest of the bench with our feet on the seat.

She looks serious.

"What's the matter, David?" It's the first thing she asks.

"I'll tell you after," I answer, because I see that she is agitated, almost as if she is angry. "What's happened to you? Something's affected you."

She looks at us both, then she lowers her gaze and after a little silence, she begins to speak.

As she does it, I note that she is sad, although she looks pretty.

She tells us what happened at home earlier with her mother. While she's telling us, her body seems very light as if she's going to fall. Her shoulders and arms seem to be weighing her down more than on other days. Her head was bent, looking down at the ground. She is angry and sad at the same time. She speaks slowly as she tells us how angry her mother became and how she was banned from entering her father's office ever again. She continues looking down at the ground. I can't see her expression and I can't see her face, only a couple of tears wetting the ground.

"You are not the only one with problems." I tell her.

I tell her what happened to my mother. She looks at me. She looks only at me as if memorising every detail of my story.

Then she comes a little closer to me and rests her head on my shoulder. I can't believe what's happening. I feel I am dying. If only she knew what emotions she's arousing in me. I smell her perfume, her warmth... her body. Please, don't let this moment end. How I love it!

Sofia looks up. As she wipes away her tears with her left sleeve, she recovers her usual decisiveness.

"After all that has happened in my house," I stand up to continue talking, "I intend to do something. This has now spread to my family and I can't stand by, with my arms folded."

I don't have to say anything more because, in the end, the same could happen to Sofia's mother or Elsa's parents tomorrow. But I can't wait any longer. We have to do something.

"I am prepared to do what Nicola says," I tell them, looking into the eyes of the two girls.

"But David," Elsa interrupts me, "all this may be a nonsense from an old madman." She falls silent for a moment and then looks down at the ground. "The problem is that, after all that has happened, we don't have many more options."

There's silence and we all look at the church wall under which a group of children are playing with a ball while their grandmothers sit on the bench next to ours.

"By the way, where is Samuel?" I ask.

"He sent a text message saying that he is going to be late," Elsa answers.

The three of us look at each other and as if in agreement, we shrug our shoulders at the same time.

The grandmothers next to us comment on how big their grandchildren are growing. At that moment, one of them faints. She appears to be asleep. Alarmed, we stand up to help her. The other women pay no attention to her, and continue as if nothing had happened. It's a false alarm. Apparently, it's normal for this lady to fall asleep in the afternoon for some minutes, her friends tell us when we show our concern.

We return to our bench.

"By the way, Sofia, you sent us a message to come here."

She looks at us for a moment and, taking out a small notebook from her backpack, she starts writing in silence. When she finishes, she shows us a succession of numbers:

"This was written on a page in my father's briefcase."

After a pause, she continues talking.

"It does not tell me anything, but the main thing is why is it only today that I discover these numbers in my father's briefcase and a photo of the little statue we saw at Nicola's house?"

One of the children comes over to collect the ball that escaped them. Elsa catches it.

"Those are Fibonacci numbers," says Elsa as she returns the ball to the child.

Sofia and I look at her, wide-eyed with surprise.

She doesn't answer immediately. She wants to create a little suspense. She looks at us and smiles mischievously when she realises that, say what you will, we are going to listen to what she has to say.

"It's very old code and it's used for many things. The sequence starts with 0 and 1, then each number is the sum of the two numbers before."

She falls silent and allows us to drill her with our expressions to continue talking. She smiles again and continues:

"The sequence has many special characteristics. As you proceed through the sequence of numbers on the list, you will find that the relationship between consecutive numbers is always the same: 1.6180 and more numbers after that. The Greeks called this relationship the PHI number and later, they called it the *golden number* or the *golden section*.

There's a strong, cold gust of wind. The children stop playing. The grandmothers are all silent. The silence at this moment is unusual. There are no cars passing.

"This relationship is the fundamental pillar of sacred geometry," Elsa finishes.

Once again, she's just managed to get my full attention. This girl is special.

"For crying out loud! Elsa, you are a walking encyclopaedia!" It was the first thing I say.

At least, I manage to make Sofia laugh a little.

Again, in less than a week, the word *geometry* makes its appearance in all of this. I see surprise more all over Sofia's face than on mine. Geometry is supposed to be her thing, but from her expression, it seems that she did not know.

"And you, how did you find out?" Sofia asks her in a tone of voice that I am unable to identify, but it isn't one of joy.

"It's part of history," Elsa answers, "and it's what I like. The PHI number comes from the Ancient Greeks. They found that, if you draw a straight line that measures PHI in two unequal parts, one of them will be one and the other is 1/PHI. It also creates other relationships." She is silent and then looks at us again directly and says: "Do you not realise it?" She speaks with such passion that you can't doubt anything she says. "It's the only number which links the small one to the large one and the large one to everything. It was a true discovery."

Elsa draws the lines and the relationships on a sheet of paper.

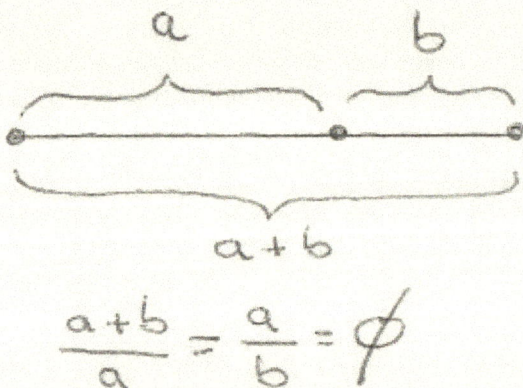

$$\frac{a+b}{a} = \frac{a}{b} = \phi$$

"I'm sorry, Elsa," Sofia says, "but I can't see the relationship between this and geometry."

"The PHI number," Elsa answers, "they call the *golden* number, and it is the basis for sacred geometry because it is in nature itself, and furthermore, it has been used for construction and architecture throughout history." She makes another drawing.

There we are, the three of us, looking at the paper on which Elsa has made a drawing, while she leans back on the backrest of the bench. In the meantime, normality has now returned to the plaza with its usual sounds. The grandmothers wake up their friend and with visible effort, they get up and call the children, motioning with their arms.

"All this is because of the way they applied this relationship between the numbers 8:5 or 13:8. In other words, they constructed geometrical figures with these relationships. For example, very few people know that the size of many objects we use nowadays bear a relationship with the golden number: tobacco packs or credit cards. But the most important thing is that there are many structures in nature itself that follow the golden number, even human DNA."

"And why did my father have this in his briefcase?" Sofia asks.

"No idea," Elsa replies.

There we are, quietly looking closely at the drawing on the paper.

After Elsa's answer, I didn't know what to say and we remain a long time in silence. I cannot bear this silence. We have to do something and soon. We are stuck, but suddenly I look up at the church again and I stare at the geometrical shapes in the high windows. I break the silence:

"Do we suppose that Emperor Augustus wanted to build a sacred city? If so, it is easy to think that he would use sacred geometry."

Seeing their faces, I feel very proud of myself. At last, it's my comment that sheds light that neither the expert in Geometry nor the expert in History has seen.

"It's very logical," Sofia says.

Then, turning to look at Elsa, I say, "Elsa, on Monday you started telling us about the life of Emperor Augustus, but you didn't finish. Could you finish telling us now?"

"Ah, yes. The most interesting thing that I was telling you is that..."

But, just at that moment, she is interrupted as Sofia stands up, looks at the church, turns around completely and stops to observe the buildings opposite the plaza. She remains pensive and watchful. With her back to the church, she starts walking towards Coso Street. She goes left and then right on the street. Then she observes the building opposite.

I admit I can't take my eyes off her. Today, she is wearing a long purple somewhat close-fitting coat and a thick woollen cream scarf which I love. But what really mesmerises me is her long, curly wind-tossed hair. Time and time again, she would move it away from her face, revealing her neck. The coppery colour of her hair shines in the sunlight and the image of her standing there, looking at the building, distracts me from everything else. She normally carries a small brown leather backpack on her shoulder. Today, she's carrying it on her arm as she's constantly taking out books and notes she has been gathering in recent days. Suddenly, I feel a tap on my arm.

"Why have you never said anything to her?" I hear Elsa's voice whispering to me.

Totally baffled and as if caught red-handed doing some childish mischief, I turn to her and ask:

"What are you talking about?"

"You know..." Elsa replies with a knowing smile. "You look miserable when you look at her. It's not the first time. I've noticed it in class."

What embarrassment! I had always thought that no one noticed it because I hid it so well. And have others also noticed it? Has Sofia? I think that I got red in the face because Elsa continues looking at me and is laughing.

"I don't know why you are telling me," I replied, looking at Sofia. "She's still going out with Erik."

There's a little silence.

"Still...?" Elsa responds and leaves me not knowing what to say.

The truth is that with the scene we saw earlier and the fuss that Erik made, it's unlikely that they are together. It was quite unpleasant. It would be difficult for them to be reconciled so soon. In fact, he's not even here.

"Hey, come on over here," Sofia shouts from where she is standing.

Both Elsa and I sit up and, circumventing the group of grandmothers and their grandchildren in the direction we are heading, we arrive at the spot where Sofia is standing. She points to the building on the other side of Coso Street and say:

"When we saw the solstice rectangle and Nicola told us the whole story, one of the things I wanted to confirm is whether the balance, that he was talking about, could have been broken because one of the reasons why the Romans built the city has not been fulfilled."

She stops because of the noise of an ambulance passing by on the street. She waits for it to pass and continues:

"That's why I've called you here and we've been checking it. According to the solstice rectangle, the winter solstice is certainly tomorrow at dawn. Presumably, the sun will light up the Eastern Gate, the entrance to the Church of La Magdalena. So, what's blocking the sun?"

We are left looking at it as if it were a riddle that we have to solve immediately.

I raise my shoulders, as does Elsa.

Sofia continues, "From what I can see, it's the buildings opposite."

We look at each other. I think she's hoping to surprise us, but nothing about this strikes a chord with me.

"But of course," Sofia continues, "it would have been there a long time ago, and the disequilibrium occurring now must be linked to something recent."

Although it seems a very logical argument, and it shows that this girl is totally caught up in the history, I don't see anything strange or special.

I look at the building she is pointing at and it is clear that it is newer than the others around it. From one end of the block to the other, there are two shops below and an entrance door more or less in the middle of the building. It has an exterior wall painted in cream, which gives it a severe look. At first, I thought that there were three floors because of the three rows of windows, but now I see that they are very long windows corresponding to only one floor. I try to discover something else that would surprise me, but there's nothing that stands out. I look at Sofia and shrug my shoulders. Elsa says nothing and waits for Sofia to continue.

"The building left me puzzled because it looked as if it had three floors, but if we look closer, we can see it has five. If we look at the buildings behind it, the older ones, they all have four floors. I have looked at the two sides of the building towards the end. Because the streets are fully aligned, they are lit up by the sun."

She remains quiet for a moment and then makes a statement:

"The buildings behind, absolutely all of them have only four floors."

She is right. I had not seen that. You have to be very observant to pick up that detail. However, I can't see how it relates to what is happening.

"You are right," I respond, "but I don't see the connection with what we are doing."

"It is because of the dawn and the time the light hits the intersection," Elsa quickly explains.

"Exactly," Sofia affirms.

I seem to be always behind them. It had never occurred to me. I look at the building again, the church, and it's possible. In fact, it can affect what Nicola told us, because part of the design of balance, supposedly planned by Augustus, was based on the light and the air entering through the *Decumanus* and it is supposed that the effect on the intersection with the *Cardus*, which he called the *Centre*, gave rise to the fifth element which he called the *Ether*. So, now if the entrance of the sun on the Centre is delayed... it could be linked.

I still don't get it.

In any case, there is something that's not adding up for me, and leaving Coso Street behind, I turn and walk towards the church. I stop immediately at the wall of the building to the left where an original stone from the Roman wall is still preserved. I see that the girls are looking at me. Now, *I* am the one who is taking his time and I move to prove something.

Let's see if Sofia is looking at me as I look at her.

I lean back against the Roman stone and turn my head to the left, in the distance, to the street that would be the *Decumanus* for the Romans and then in the opposite direction towards the building Sofia pointed out. Seeing me do this, the two girls come towards me. Sofia is still looking at me.

"And..?"

I already feel a little better. Again, I've just done something that had not occurred to her and she's even interested in what I say. I wish the world would stop for a few minutes for me to savour the moment, with the girl I like standing very near me, looking and expecting me to discover something.

After a few fractions of a second, I can see that the world is certainly not going to stop. What a pity, how I would have enjoyed it! I answer quickly so as not to cause discomfort.

So, I start by saying, "From here, the sun should enter the *Decumanus*. I don't believe that the entrance to the church marks the direction through which the sun has to enter, but rather the ancient gate, which is the street itself. What is certain is that this last stone, which is all that remains from the original wall, must be the place where the gate started for the sunlight to enter."

From Sofia's face, I can see that it had not occurred to her because she seriously looks at one side and then at the other, until she finally makes a gesture of agreement. So, I continue:

"As you can see, the building to the left blocks the light even though it only has four or five floors."

I move aside for them to check it. I see that Sofia doesn't agree. So, she moves around and looks at one side and then the other. After a while, she crosses Coso Street and walks towards the building and checks its sides, observing everything around it.

Suddenly, she stops and faces the church, towards where we are standing. She is looking at the church, with her eyes fixed on the top of the building. She puts her hand into the backpack, and both Elsa and I are amazed when she takes out small binoculars. After a while, she lowers her gaze and looks at us. I see a slight smile on her face. She crosses the street together with a group of grandparents at the lights.

When she gets back to us, she looks at me and says:

"I think you are right and the clue appears to be in the way the light enters the street, and so it does not appear that the height of the building has any effect...

She remains silent trying to imbue some mystery and then continues:

"... but I don't know if we can explain why, in the roof of this church, someone has constructed a small arch, in the form of the ancient gate drawn on the painting we saw earlier." And she points at the wall on the left on the other side of the street from the church.

Just at that moment, we are startled. There, standing on the other side of the street like an apparition, is Samuel with his customary long coat and the brightest trainers in the world. Hands in pockets, he watches us with an expressionless face.

CHAPTER 25

Thursday 22 December 2016
Time: 5:00 pm

Sofia

I had never imagined what I was getting myself into. It is difficult for me to make a decision because deep down all this seems to be based on something that is so imaginative that could only happen in films.

After checking the entrance of the light onto the street and on the church for some time, we've returned to our bench.

Standing by my side, Samuel has taken out his tablet and has written down something. The three of us are wondering about the reason he has given for not arriving at the same time as the rest of us. 'He had to do things' is the only explanation he gave us. And of course, who is going to ask him 'what things'? Who dares to get involved in his mysterious life? At the end of the day, that's how he is and we're not going to change him. There's something in him that inspires both respect and affection in me. Since the incident in the ice cream parlour, I've noticed that the others treat him better. I've always got on well with him, but I notice now that there is a greater rapport with the whole group.

I glance at him and smile without him realising that I'm looking at him.

Elsa and David are sitting on the backrest of the bench with their feet on the seat. I prefer standing because with the way the wind is blowing today, I can use both hands to smooth my hair each time the wind lifts it. Elsa has short hair and doesn't need to. So she can use her hands to secure herself on the bench.

"I think," I begin to say, "that we can agree that all this seems rather ridiculous, but at the same time there's information that is taking us around the problem. But what is a fact is that people are losing their balance... Are we going to do it!"

The three of us look at each other in silence. Elsa turns her head towards the church which, at that moment, is in the shade. The three long windows in the facade observe us in silence as if waiting for us to guess their secret.

"After what has happened to my mother," David adds in a serious and determined voice, "it's very clear to me that we have to carry on with what we are doing."

The three of us look at Elsa, as she continues to observe the top of the church. She still has not yet seen the small 'gate' in the roof, but I am sure that she is now curious.

I explained all to Samuel when he arrived and he has seen it immediately. That is when he took out his tablet to take notes.

Elsa is now watching us in silence. It's an uncomfortable silence because neither David nor I dare to interrupt her.

"I, too, think that something is happening and we have to act," Elsa continues, "but before we do, I would like to confirm some information at home tonight."

She looks at the three of us again and says:

"But in answer to your question, the answer is yes..., but we have to prepare well for it."

She stops for a moment.

I love it when she has her pensive face on, looking up with her fingers touching her bottom lip. If anyone made a sculpture of her, I'm sure they would put it in a museum. She looks inspired.

The time has come to start making decisions. I have to start moving things along.

"From what Nicola told us," Samuel surprises us all, "what we need now is the music."

He manages to attract our attention from the couple kissing on the bench next to us. All at once, we turn to look at him, frowning as if he reminded us of something that they told us when we were children. Since we left the old man's house, no one has mentioned it. He's taken us by surprise.

But he continues to look at his tablet and says nothing more.

I break the ice, "For the portal to open, Nicola said that at a certain time on the dot, a specific music must be played. Otherwise, it will not do..." I hesitate because I notice that the three of them are looking behind me, and David's expression changes completely. I continue what I am saying, "... this is a momentous occasion. We are on the point of making a decision to embark on something that we have never imagined, and here we go!"

But just as I finish my sentence, I turn around and I find Erik standing and staring at me.

Although I am angry with him, I have to admit that he is one attractive guy. He's wearing tight jeans with the ends tucked into the beige-coloured boots he's put on today. He's wearing a black woollen coat and the same white scarf he was wearing when we went to the museum. But today his hands are in his pockets, and to protect himself from the cold wind, he's put on a Nordic woollen cap, which looks good on him. I am dumbstruck. I can only stare at him. I feel my heart pounding. I would shout at him right now for behaving so badly earlier, and at the same time I want to hug him for a long time, to feel his arms around me. But I do nothing. I just stare at him.

Suddenly, he breaks the silence:

"Before going anywhere..." He is quiet for a moment and then looks into my eyes: "... we have to talk."

What a most unpleasant situation! I turn and see Elsa smiling at us. David, on the other hand, turns pale and avoids my gaze. He holds his hands so tightly as if he wanted to squeeze his fingers. I've only seen him like this once in class when the teacher asked him a question. When I turned around, I saw that he was nervous. I would like to ask him what's the matter. I would like to continue with what we were talking about, but at the moment I am in a dilemma. I don't know what to do.

"I'm going." David suddenly stands up and picks up his bag.

I see Elsa taking his arm to slow him down, and with her other hand makes a sign to Samuel above his tablet.

"The rest of us have to go too," she says, standing next to them and positioning us as if to form a circle of the five, she continues, "If you want, we can get together online tonight and share whatever we have. I think I know where I have to look for what I need. See you soon."

The three of them leave. Elsa has taken David's arm, but he doesn't say good bye. I don't know what's the matter with him. Samuel walks alongside them, but a couple of metres apart.

"Let's walk," Erik says quite seriously.

He starts walking down the street to the left of the Church of La Magdalena towards the Calle Mayor. I walk beside him.

If anyone had said this to me and in this way at any other time, I would simply tell him to leave me in peace. But this time, I agree. If he wants to apologise for his behaviour earlier, I am not going to make it more difficult for him. I imagine that it's not easy for him to do it.

After going across St Vincent de Paul Street, we head for Calle Mayor, but specifically to the intersection where I was earlier, before meeting up with the others, and where I had begun to relax among the crowd.

The Calle Mayor is somewhat special for me because it gives access to two of the plazas I like most in the city. One is the Plaza Santa Maria, where you can get some of the best *tapas* and enjoy a historical spot which has not lost its ancient knowledge. The other is the Plaza San Pedro Nolasco. We are heading towards it. As we cross Argensola Street, we turn left to go across this plaza.

It seems difficult for him to talk because during the time we've been walking, he has not said anything. And what is strange for him is that he has not taken his hands out of his pockets.

In Plaza San Pedro Nolasco, I've enjoyed very good open-air concerts on ancient music, organised for the festivals in the city. But today I'm not thinking of that as we walk along the street.

As we come to the end of Argensola Street, and before entering the plaza, I look to my right, where the Roman ruins of the ancient baths have been preserved. These ruins now hold another meaning for me with all that we are immersed in. The most special thing is that I am very close to the two most important preserved Roman ruins. The other is the amphitheatre which we are going to come across as we continue walking straight down the street to the end, with the church on the right. I glance across at Erik and I see that he is still looking down at the ground as he is walking.

As we continue further along Pedro Joaquín Soler Street, the full expanse of the old Roman amphitheatre opens up on our right. Erik stops, leans against the fence, facing the interior and without looking at me, begins to talk.

"What I am going to tell you is somewhat more incredible than all that we've been talking about until now."

Well! Well! Well! I thought he was going to apologise. Although I must admit that he's grabbed my attention.

"...the problem is that you may not be ready to hear it."

Well, who would believe it? Not only does he not apologise, but he also treats me like a child. Then, he turns to me, puts his hands on my shoulders, and looks into my eyes.

"Are you ready to listen to something that is going to change your life?"

For some seconds, I don't know what to say. Then, I simply nodded.

CHAPTER 26

Thursday 22 December 2016
Time: 6 pm

David

The best thing I can do is to stop being mortified. It's happened and can't be changed. I think it's one of the best lessons I've learnt in life and today, in particular, I have to remember it.

After Erik arrived at Plaza de la Magdalena, Samuel hurriedly said goodbye and went home. Elsa was very friendly on the way back as we walked along together until she said goodbye to go home. I'm not accustomed to a girl taking my arm, but with Elsa it didn't bother me because I look upon her as a good friend and she knows about my feelings for Sofia. I keep asking myself how she found out, but as my friend Jon says, often the face expresses what the soul feels and we can't control that.

In the end, I called my Uncle Daniel from my mobile while I was walking home. I asked after my mother and my brother. He told me that she had woken up, but was very tired and fell asleep again. I told him that I'll stay home. He insisted that I should go over to his house, but after I explained that I had something important to do, he relented.

I've always had a special connection with my uncle. From the time I was small, we would often look at each other and I think that we knew what each other was thinking. My mother recognised it and with the loss of my father, I've come to realise that she has tried to keep the relationship with my uncle and his family alive. I don't believe that she expected something to happen to her or that we would have to ask for help. Or perhaps she did, and is that the reason why she had a talk with us the night before? It doesn't matter now. I have to make my own decisions and fortunately, we have Uncle Daniel to support us.

Elsa's suggestion to remain in our own homes to get more information was a very good idea. I think each of us needs to be alone, to reflect and put our ideas in order. Well, I have no idea what Samuel will do. He continues being an unknown factor to me. In the case of Sofia and Erik, perhaps they have other plans, but I've decided to forget about that and concentrate on the 'jump'.

As always, the computer takes a while to turn on, each time I press the switch button, it takes more time than before. I remain watching the screen as a lot of dialogue boxes open, they are visible for a while, then they say that the task is completed and finally close. And then there is another and another. While I watch it, I blame myself for its slowness because the computer technicians always say that it depends on the number of programmes you download onto your computer. The more there are and stored I don't know where, the more slowly the computer will run. Next week, I am going to delete programmes.

I feel the silence at home. Deep down, it's uncomfortable because the reason for it is not good. I hope my mother is well. I am sure that Marco will be having a great time with the cousins. I think deep down, he likes the youngest. But, after all, we are family.

My room is tidy. The truth is that the whole house is always tidy. My mother insists upon it and we dare not disobey her. Therefore my light brown desk does not have any paper on it. It is all stored in the drawers below, even my pens. I think that, of all the people in my class, I must be the only one with such a clear table.

What would impress a stranger to our home about my room is how simple it is. I have the bed behind me; opposite, the table with an enormous mirror in which I look at myself all the time; and a wardrobe on the right. On my left, the window allows full sunlight into the room because, a couple of years ago, I decided not to put up any curtains or venetian blinds that would block the view of the large tree on the street in front. Living on the third floor, I have a full view of the branches and leaves of the tree. I love it.

At last, the laptop is on. The Wi-Fi connection is good and all is ready. I look at my hands. They are not like Nicola's. Mine normally touch the keys on the keyboard and pens for working. How times have changed! Years ago, boys my age were already working with tools, helping their parents in the countryside and doing various manual jobs. "This is all part of technological advancement," I say to myself each time I make the comparison. I stretch my fingers in a sort of ceremony before the computer and, with a speed that amazes my companions, I start conducting my search on the Internet.

The first thing I do is to open the new application that we have been sharing in class. It operates like a videoconferencing tool on which six people can be online at the same time and see each other's faces, one at every corner of the screen. We can automatically share files, information and in particular, websites for us to undertake a proper search. I have to send an invitation to the five of us although, at this moment, inviting Erik is one thing I absolutely don't care to do.

Elsa accepts the invitation immediately and I can see her on the screen:

"Hello, here I am," she greets me.

"One moment, I'm going to adjust the sound on the speakers," I respond. Normally, I have it adjusted for headphones, but as I am alone today, I prefer to use the speakers."

"I can hear you now and I can see you very well," Elsa replies.

I adjust the speakers, the volume and the brightness on the screen. Elsa is in her room and is wearing a light-coloured blouse, and so I can see her face very well. If my mum were here, she would be commenting on how untidy my schoolmates' rooms are. But, this is not the time to think of my mother.

"Perfect, Elsa. I can hear you loud and clear."

Without saying anything more to each other, just seeing each other at the edge of the screen, we begin to type on the computer. From the sound on the keys, I recognise that we are both surfing the Internet. I am aware that unless one of us finds something really interesting, we won't say anything to each other. Up to this moment, the only sound is the sound of the keys. Neither Samuel, Sofia nor Erik is on the screen. They haven't accepted the invitation.

Suddenly, there is the sound that someone else has gone online and has connected with us. But there is no picture of them.

"Hello," I say in the silence of my room. "Who's there?"

I hear a strange noise on the speakers, like someone scratching a metal surface. It's a grating noise. How unpleasant!

"Who's there?" I repeat when I don't hear a response.

"Hello." I can now recognise Samuel's voice. "Everything fell on the floor, the mouse and the keyboard."

"I thought that someone was scratching something." I hear Elsa's voice on the speakers.

"Yes, well..." Samuel starts, "It was one of the cats. He was trying to draw a circle on the computer screen."

"Ow," Elsa says again.

"Ah, no harm done!" Samuel answers as if there was a question that required him to say something. "I have a screen protector which I change every month."

I notice that he has not activated the video, only the audio. The only thing I see on screen is the photo that he posted up to introduce himself. Although I must say that instead of a photo, it's a drawing. On a black background he has a drawing of the symbol of infinity in yellow, the typical number eight lying on its side. I've no idea why he's put up that drawing and I imagine that he's not activated the video because he doesn't want us to see his house. I imagine that it is small, poor, with many people living together. Why did I say that? Sometimes, I feel ashamed of my thoughts.

I will focus on what I have to do.

I know where to begin. I type in 'ashlar at Valencia Gate'. Many web addresses appear and I quickly try to see if there's anything special. In my opinion, the ashlar is the start of all of this because Sofia was observing it when the guide approached her in the museum. Then, it was on one of the documents in her father's briefcase. So, there must be something there.

After searching for a while, I stumble across the same translation from Latin of the letters visible on the left side of the ashlar. They all make reference to the words, 'Those who built the gate may they return to their country'. Within this fanciful scenario, it is the only thing that makes reference to a possible 'journey' through the portal.

Introduce the same words in Spanish, French and also in Italian, 'these marvellous online translators'. It is when I type in 'Roman gate' in Italian, something new appears.

"I think that I've found something," I say on the microphone and I heard Elsa stop typing on the computer. "I am sending you the website address."

A few seconds afterwards, Elsa answers:

"I've received it and I am opening it." She is quiet for a moment and continues. "This is new. Guardian gods? What is this?" I notice that she is skimming the document and then she says: "I'll start with this."

I have no idea what 'this' is. I leave her to do the research. I found it in a study by a History teacher at a university in Madrid, and it is precisely all about the ashlar. It's incredible that someone has been able to do research only on this stone. But, I am not surprised because I am totally intrigued, not so much by the translations, but by the right side which is impossible to read. How could someone do something like that? They left the letters on the left although not all can be seen. On the right, they carved something. Then, they 'defaced'

181

it, or as they say when someone tries to erase what has been carved.

"Do you see anything?" I ask.

"Yes," Elsa answers, reading as she speaks. "Here, there is another translation of the letters on the left side of the ashlar. I'll write them out for you."

I hear her typing on the computer and finally she presses a key which I imagine is *Enter*. Thereupon, I receive the following text:

'(This is the) Gate of Rome: Let the people who built it work and bring offerings to (the images of) the guardian gods'.

"Caesar, (son) of the divine..."

I read it and ask: "What does it mean?"

"I have no idea," replied Elsa.

Then, at this moment, my mobile rings. I look at the screen. It's Sofia. My heart skips a beat. I noticed that Elsa and Samuel have stopped typing. I can only hear the sound of my telephone.

"Hi, how are you?" I ask amiably.

"Are you alone at home?" Sofia asked. If it was cold, I am now freezing.

"Yes."

"Would you mind if we came over to you. I am with Erik and we are close to your apartment. It's best for me to tell you what I know and let us do the search quickly."

False alarm! She's back with Erik. I can't think about that now. We have to focus on the 'jump'. It does not make sense that they are close to my home because neither of them lives in this area. I don't understand.

"No problem." I answer. "How long will it take you to get here?"

"No time at all. We're outside."

At that moment, the doorbell rings.

CHAPTER 27

Thursday 22 December 2016
Time: 6:30 pm

Sofia

I've been standing for at least 15 minutes on the other side of the front door of my home. It's difficult for me to open it. I can't even bring myself to put the key into the keyhole because this simple detail would activate the springs in my mother's very fine hearing. Anyone seeing me would think that I was mad. They would have observed me, with keys in my hand, just looking at the keyhole and leaning against the front door through which I pass everyday without question.

The problem is that when I open and enter the apartment, I don't know what to say. Perhaps, I could go to my room without saying anything to anyone. Or, I could go to whatever room my mother is in and tell her what I think of her and use all the words she calls 'bad words', one after the other, until she understood how badly she made me feel. Perhaps I could forget the last ban she gave me and head directly for my father's office, open the door and rummage as much as I like.

I could demand answers to all that Erik had begun to tell me.

In the end, I couldn't open the door and therefore went over to Erik's house instead. Who would have said a few weeks ago that I was going to do what I've just done. My mum will never know. If she ever finds out, I will not be able to explain it to her.

It's done.

Now, I have to muster up all my strength to go up these stairs. I feel weary. I only have two more floors to go up before I press the door bell that always looks so new, always so clean and orderly as the inside of his apartment.

I can't get it out of my mind. I can only think about what Erik told me before in the street. It was all so incredible. It must have been difficult for him to tell me, although on top of that, I can imagine how difficult it was, first of all, to believe it.

After the spectacle he created, going off in such an ill-mannered way in the middle of the street, he ended up going directly home. According to what he told me, he threw himself down on the sofa without turning on the TV and remained staring up at the ceiling for a long time until his mother came over to talk to him. It was the first time she has seen him so worried and sad. So, Erik did not mind trying to alleviate her concerns and answered her questions. It seems that he hadn't told them about going out with a girl and that he was angry with her (I don't think that I would have liked that because I regarded him differently, but I let him continue without interrupting).

I don't know when or why he mentioned my name and my full surname:

"Sofia Canizzaro."

His mother's expression changed completely and then she asked him:

"Do you know her father's name?"

According to Erik, he remembered because he knew that my surname was Italian since my father was the son of immigrants and, although I had mentioned my dad's first name only once, he remembered it from the first time he heard it as he thought that it was such an unusual name. He knew that it wasn't a common name in Zaragoza, but in other places it is.

"Augustus."

His mother became really nervous. She turned white, raising her hands to her mouth. Erik had never seen her so frightened before. Her habit of passing her hand over her hair when she was serious must have turned to that unconscious habit of squeezing it as if trying to wring it. She quickly went to call her husband and the two of them sat down with Erik. He told me that he forgot his anger when he saw his parents reacting in this way.

I've only been to his home once. They have furniture commonly seen in Swedish shops, in very light colours, bleached almost to whiteness, but without being white. I can imagine him lying on the sofa, with eyes lost on the bookshelves opposite, full, or rather crowded with books, without a coffee table between the sofa and the bookshelves. His parents sat on two chairs in front of him so that he could look at them directly.

And now, here I am, on the other hand, entering David's house with Erik to tell him, Samuel and Elsa, who are most certainly linked up for videoconferencing, about what has happened.

CHAPTER 28

Thursday 22 December 2016
Time: 7:00 pm

David

The madness is now gathering pace. Furthermore, the deadline Nicola gave us is fast coming to an end. We only have a few hours to the dawn of the winter solstice and we're not fully prepared.

After listening to Sofia, everything makes sense. We've decided to act immediately. The three of us are in the living room, around the large dark mahogany table my parents bought when they got married. Sofia has begun to do an Internet search on my brother's computer, while Erik works on his tablet. I don't know how he did it, but Samuel appeared at my apartment two minutes after I opened for Sofia and Erik. I imagine that he must have heard me talking to Sofia on the phone when she told me that they were coming over to my home. But, how was he able to come so quickly? Well, I don't really know where he lives, so I don't know if he was fast or slow. He connected a small wireless keyboard to the tablet he always carries in his backpack and now he is busy tapping away on the keyboard. Elsa is connected via video and we've already identified several things, but I am going very slowly.

Erik has begun to tell us what happened at his home with his parents, until he told them Sofia's father's name.

"... and I told him not to tell me anything more." Sofia rouses me from my thoughts."

"How you mean 'not to tell you anything more'?" Elsa asks.

"She asked me if it was linked to what was happening to us these days in the city," Erik replied, looking at Elsa, or rather her image on the screen.

Although the four of us are around the living room table, I have connected my laptop to the system we have at home via the Wi-Fi, which links the audio feed to the sound equipment and projects the video onto the wall above the sofa through a cable we put up on the ceiling. I think it's a very good device which they started selling this year and, as my mother is an IT expert, she always likes having the latest gadgets in the market.

"Are you OK with all of us listening to it?" We hear Elsa's words resounding through the living room.

Sofia doesn't answer, but nods her head in agreement.

"Could you start?" Samuel takes us by surprise with his question, as he stands up, goes to the armchair under the window and, with an uncharacteristic elegance, he sits down slowly. With hands resting on the arms of the chair and tilting his head a little, he looks directly up at Erik.

The three of us look at each other in amazement. He looks almost comical, with his large overcoat open to reveal black trousers and a black jumper. It's strange because I've always imagined him to be a bigger guy, but with the close-fitting jumper he is wearing today, I realise that he is quite slim. We've always seen him in overcoats and baggy clothes, and so he's created a very different image from what I'm seeing today, especially as his coat has some stains on the sleeves, making him look untidy.

He puts his feet together, which seems almost exaggerated as he sits with his knees together. Who sits like that?

"What's happening?" We hear Elsa's voice.

No one answers. Samuel continues looking at Erik.

"Helloooo," We hear Elsa's voice again.

"Nothing's happening, Elsa," I answer. "It seems that our friend Samuel has something to tell us."

The three of us turn to look at him. He looks different.

"I prefer Erik to tell us what he wants to say," Samuel interrupts with a slight smile.

"What are you on about?" Erik asks, "Do you know something that you want to tell us?"

Erik stands up and leans on the back of the chair. He looks at Samuel in a defiant way.

187

"I know that your parents didn't come here only for the sun and the wind," Samuel replies.

His words resound throughout the room. Even the expression on Elsa's face projected on the wall undergoes a change. Erik walks over to Samuel. I don't like his attitude. I stand up and go between them.

"Shall we all sit down?" "Darn it!" Sofia shouts.

Good God! What a reaction! I think that it is the first time I've heard her say a bad word. Has super-polite Sofia discovered her more unpleasant inner self when she becomes agitated? Or is it what Erik has told her, that is beginning to change her? He turns towards her and looks at her wide-eyed as I have never seen him do before. You could cut the silence with a knife. Samuel has not even batted an eye. Elsa, on the screen, looks paralysed. I sit down. Erik does the same.

"Samuel, can you tell us," Sofia begins, speaking to him slowly, articulating her words in a tone that no longer reflects as much congeniality as before, "what you know?" She stops for a moment to look at Erik, "And why you know it?"

CHAPTER 29

Thursday 22 December 2016
Time: 7:30 pm

Sofia

It's happened to me again! How can I utter such a bad word?

First, I shout an insult at my mother at home and again, the same thing is happening. What's happening to me? I've always had the reputation of being the most polite. My parents have brought me up like that, but... everything is changing, and I am too. I like being quick, for everything to happen quickly: to make one decision after another. But I cannot lose respect for others. This whole problem is overwhelming me.

Samuel has succeeded in making us all focus on him. I thought that he was one of those freaks who want to pass unnoticed and perhaps that was why I wanted to befriend him; that and because no one wanted to be with him. The long overcoat he always wears gives him a sinister look. Today, however, I've noticed that he's well-groomed again. I think that's the second time I've seen him like this.

"Sorry," Samuel starts, speaking softly and looking down at the floor.

The guys move chairs around as if they didn't know where to put themselves.

"I think I should be there!" I hear Elsa's voice.

I cross my arms on the table and look directly at Samuel's face.

"Erik's parents belong to *Disequilibriums.*"

That I did not expect. But what is he talking about? Erik abruptly jumps to his feet.

"And, how do you know this?"

Well, this is all becoming very exciting. The truth, I mean. His parents belong to something that I don't know what it is.

Is this what he was going to tell me, what I prevented him from saying unless the five of us were together? And now, how's this going to turn out? I'm accustomed to making quick decisions, but on this occasion, I have to stand aside. They have to resolve this conflict themselves.

Erik is totally flushed. His fists are clenched. As he had rolled up his sleeves earlier, I can see the tension in his arm muscles. They are like rope. I've never seen him like this. He looks as if he is about to explode.

"Jävla skit!" He shouts. *"Jävla skit!*[1] *"*

As he says it, he begins to calm down. I don't know what it means, but it seems to calm him.

"Right now," Erik starts speaking, looking at the table, "I don't care what you know and how you know it. I wanted to tell Sofia for some time, but she decided that I had to do it in front of you."

He stands up slowly. He must have changed again as he's wearing light brown corduroy trousers which match his boots. Over his beige tee-shirt, he's wearing a typical woodcutter's overshirt with large red and white squares. As he reaches the window and looks out at the tree outside, he looks as if he is in the woods about to start his work. The only thing missing is the axe. With his hands in his pockets and leaning a little against the glass, he starts speaking.

"It is true. Today, I found out that my parents didn't come here to live in this city only because of the wind and sun. There was another reason."

This is new! Darn it! Every minute is taking on a new dimension. I am seriously regretting not listening to him before coming here.

Samuel gets up from the armchair and comes over to sit next to David and me around the table.

---

[1]Shit (translation from Swedish).

190

"According to what they told me," Erik continues, "both belong to a group which has been spreading to many cities worldwide for the last two years."

"It all started," Samuel interrupts him and all of us, except Erik, turn to look at him, "when someone launched the idea in 2011 that this world crisis was different from all the others."

"Look," Erik continues, without looking away from the window and with a slow but serious voice, "I don't know how you know, but as I've started, I prefer you let me finish."

Samuel nods, without saying a word.

"This person," Erik continues, "launched the idea that this crisis is the consequence of some imbalance: an imbalance or disequilibrium occurring in nature itself, with the widespread plunder of raw materials, pollution, use of water resources, a social and economic disequilibrium and above all, something which he calls *Integral disequilibrium*."

He stops for a moment and turning towards us, he says:

"This last kind of imbalance, according to the group, has played a significant part in the crisis which started off as a financial one, leading to the terrible social repercussions we are currently experiencing."

He returns to sit with us around the table.

"To find out the causes for this imbalance, that person went to research it in recorded history, specifically the history of Europe, from the ancient Greeks and Romans. And that was when he found out what we have discovered in recent days."

"The geometrical arrangement of the city of Zaragoza and its links to the sun," Samuel interrupts him again, but this time, Erik takes no offense.

"According to what my parents told me," Erik continues, "all the research is based on how the design of the city is linked to some supposed balance and how that could affect its inhabitants. Furthermore, how this balance created by Romans with the *Cardus* and *Decumanus* affected everything else."

"And who organised everything?" Elsa asks.

191

"Wait!" Erik continues, looking at Elsa's image on the wall, "the first thing this person did was to share what he had found out through his networks and then he founded the group."

"But," David asks interestedly, "who are the people in this group?"

"Mainly they were people who lived in cities where the city design was based on *Cardus* and *Decumanus*. One would never have imagined that there would be so many, not only in Europe, but also in North Africa, in South America and several major cities in the United States where they have this design."

"So," I say the first thing that occurs to me, "they are like a sect."

Erik frowns and crosses his arms on the table. I don't think my comment was appropriate.

"No, it is not a sect or a secret society." I think that he's a bit annoyed. I will not interrupt again. "They are simply a working group made up of various people who've started to share how their cities overcame past crises, how we could overcome this one and how we could prevent another from happening."

"What's the name of the group?" David asks.

Erik looks up at Samuel and nods.

"Disequilibriums," Samuel answers.

So that was the name of the group! When he mentioned it before, Samuel didn't know what it referred to. I see from the faces of the others that we are all looking at him in jaw-dropping amazement.

"Like any other group on social networks," Erik continues quickly, "they had to give themselves a name and this was it. Almost all of them were professionals in different fields, not only historians. Filled with the desire to combine their efforts for a common purpose, they began to work together. There was no administration, other than for each person to contribute information they found, share it and together improve it and try to design what they all agreed to call 'the guide to balance'.

"I can't hear you," Elsa complained. "Can you speak more loudly please? Or close to the mike?"

As we are doing the video from his computer, David put his laptop close to Erik.

"The guide to balance," Erik repeats and looks at Elsa's image until she nods.

"There is something I don't understand." We can hear Elsa's voice again.

"What?" I notice that Erik's voice sounds a little irritated at being interrupted.

"When he mentioned it earlier, Samuel raised a question in my mind and while you were all speaking, I checked the English dictionaries."

In silence, we watch as Elsa's image, projected on the wall, turn the pages of the book in her hands.

"The word 'disequilibriums' does not exist," she continues, "The plural of 'disequilibrium' is 'disequilibria'.

I love my friend. Always the perfectionist.

We all turn to Erik, waiting for his response in silence.

"You are certainly observant, Elsa", he responds. "You are right. As my father was explaining this part of the story, my mother affectionately interrupted him to tell him this."

"Well done you, Elsa!" David exclaimed, thrilled with what is taking place. How I enjoy watching him when he is happy!

"According to what they told me," Erik continues, "'disequilibria' is the name they were going to use, but they realised that it was already being used on social networks for other things. So, despite having a linguist in the group, they all agreed to use a word with which, although it did not exist, they could still reserve URL domains on the Internet."

Samuel's face is amusing. He must have searched on his tablet and is now looking at the screen, nodding in agreement.

"Yes, it's true," he said in a low voice. "I didn't know that."

I think that he felt disappointed with himself for not having discovered it before. I love it. We're discovering a little more about each other all the time.

David pats him on the back a couple of times and smiles.

"I can tell you," Erik continues, "that, when my parents began to talk to me about this, they became excited. They kept on interrupting each other, but always to add something new to what was said earlier. They did not get angry with each other, which normally happens when they are discussing other things, whenever one starts something and the other interrupts.

"How long have they been doing this?" I ask him, interested.

"The work started a year ago. They joined in Sweden, not because their city had been designed with a *Cardus* and a *Decumanus*, but because they worked on projects to use the air and sun in their country, and on one of the social networks in which they were connected to other members of the group working on the concept of *balance* through the four elements of nature: air, water, earth and fire.

"But something changed, didn't it?" Samuel asked.

CHAPTER 30

Thursday 22 December 2016
Time: 8:00 pm

David

I don't know what surprised me more, the story itself or the fact that Samuel knew about it. After a moment of tension, the atmosphere improves. I feel relaxed enough to hear something that has impressed me. I like this kind of intrigue. It's almost like a film.

I thought that Sofia was going to intervene, but surprisingly, she is not taking the initiative. If it were any other moment in the past, I bet she would have been directing the show. I don't know what is the matter with her. In any case, she looks very pretty.

"Yes, Samuel," Erik continues, "before summer 2015, the Disequilibriums Group had a major about-turn in the research they were doing and sharing."

"What happened?" I couldn't help asking.

"The initiator launched the idea that Zaragoza was the sacred city and, in particular, about the tilted *Cardus* and *Decumanus*. That shook up the group. According to what my parents told me, from that moment, the volume of communications traffic among group members increased by 100% and many people started having more meetings, even some members in Asia."

"Wow!!!" We can hear Elsa exclaiming. "How I would have liked to experience that!"

Without realising it, she voiced what the rest of us are thinking, but none dares to say.

"From that moment, my parents began to work harder because they were the ones who informed the group that in Paris, the same thing was happening."

"In Paris?" Startled, Samuel springs into action, reaching for his tablet to search for something on the Internet.

I notice a slight smile on Erik's face. Here's something that Samuel didn't know. He is full of pride.

"From that moment, they got into direct contact with the initiator of the group: Augustus Canizzaro."

I look at Sofia. Her face undergoes a mixture of expressions and feelings that are impossible to interpret. She shifts uncomfortably in her seat. She tries to find a comfortable position, but cannot. Finally, she stands up and goes over to sit on the armchair where Samuel had been sitting previously.

"From what they told me, it seems that my parents established a very close relationship with Sofia's father."

"Dear me! What are you saying?" Sofia asks in alarm.

No one says anything. Erik and Sofia are locked in a gaze. She turns white, with wide unblinking eyes. His face is a mixture of sadness and fear. I think that he is wondering whether to continue or to stop.

Sofia suddenly recovers. She blinks quickly and with a slight movement of her head, she looks at all of us. Finally, she turns to fix her eyes on Erik and, as if expected, she gives him the nod to continue.

"Later they told me," Erik begins and stops for a moment until Sofia, with a nod, motions for him to continue, "that Sofia's mother played an important role, but they could not yet reveal it."

Sofia's jaw drops. Erik gestures to her to ask if he should continue the story. She gets up again, approaches the table, returns to sit on the chair she had been sitting on previously, covers her face with her hands and rubs it. Then, with her face now clear, she turns to him and gestures for him to continue.

"That special relationship arose because Disequilibriums became more powerful since many people who lived or have lived in cities designed with a *Cardus* and *Decumanus* seem to be more predisposed to finding solutions aimed at establishing balance."

Erik adopts a more rigid position and lifts his head and, looking straight ahead, continues:

"Just before summer, Sofia's father informed my parents that, on their family holidays, and by pure chance, he had found three more cities in Europe where the *Cardus* and *Decumanus* were tilted: London, Paris and Bergamo. However, in none of them was the solstice rectangle exactly the same as in Zaragoza."

"What did you say?" We can hear Elsa asking.

Erik turns towards the screen, and cupping his mouth like a loudspeaker, he repeats:

"LONDON, PARIS AND BERGAMO.

"Tell me this isn't happening," Sofia groans as if from the depths of her being.

"In fact, in Paris," Erik continues, "there are several *Decumanus* and one main *Cardus*. One of the people who joined the group commented that, depending on the *Decumanus* you choose, with one end in Montmartre and the other in Montparnasse, the Notre-Dame Cathedral could be identified as the intersection."

Samuel takes up the story, "From London, one of the members of the group showed the Roman design of the city and, although it is true that the *Cardus* and *Decumanus* were tilted, they were not totally straight as in other cities, but what stood out was their position relative to the River Thames."

Erik makes a sign to Samuel to stop speaking and he continues:

"And the third city that Augustus Canizzaro found to have a tilted *Cardus* and *Decumanus* was Bergamo, a small Italian city, near Milan. He had to be very observant to find it, but as the old town is very well preserved, the tower at the intersection of the two lines enabled him to find the connection."

"We went to the three cities for two summers running," Sofia cuts in, covering her eyes with her hands.

I can't begin to imagine what's going through Sofia's head.

197

With a small smile at Sofia, Erik continues, "Last summer, all the members of Disequilibriums knew where Augustus Canizzaro was spending his family holidays. He told them that he had planned to do a series of actions in each of the three cities."

Samuel puts his hands on the table and says:

"I only know up to this point, but not the rest."

We took no notice of Samuel. We want Erik to continue and I imagine Sofia will want to know how it was.

"The problem emerged after summer. Communications from Augustus Canizzaro reduced in volume. That did not mean that the group stopped working. It was a special group because it did its work online and if a member was not there or was missing, the group itself would pick up the slack and reinforce the areas where that member was working."

He then points to his tablet where he had put up photos of the pictures Sofia had found in her father's briefcase.

"Between summer and Christmas last year, the two communications that Sofia's father sent referred to a *sacred geometry*."

"What?" Elsa and I utter at the same time.

We've only just discovered these references! We are getting increasingly close to the problem. I glance at Samuel. I notice a slight gesture as he opened his eyes wide, which I'm sure he would never admit. But I would never be able to prove it as immediately, in a matter of seconds, he returned to his neutral expression. What a strange guy. From being a major player on the armchair, he is now a passive figure sitting at the table.

"But here's the most shocking detail," says Erik, looking directly at Sofia.

She's been behaving rather strangely for some time. She keeps touching her hair. With her face fully illuminated by the light entering through the window, she looks pretty. What am I thinking? I have zero possibilities, after seeing the reconciliation between them. I give up... at least for the moment.

"My parents did research on this and tried to contact Augustus, but to no avail, and since 23rd December 2015, they haven't heard anything more from him."

Good God! What a moment! That was the day Sofia's father disappeared. She buries her face in her hands and rests her head on the table. No one says anything. Even Samuel is looking at her. I turn to look at the wall and at Elsa's image moving aimlessly from side to side. She does this when she is nervous.

"So, they decided to come to Zaragoza to try to trace him," Sofia summarises, still with her face in her hands, but loud enough for us to hear her.

"In fact," Samuel stuns us all, speaking at this very special moment, "they met several times with Sofia's mother."

Any sign of friendliness vanished from Sofia and Erik's faces at the same time. They look wide-eyed at the one who, for some strange reason, decided to comb his hair.

"Better explain yourself because I'm really getting angry," Sofia demands.

With his hands, Samuel motions to Sofia to calm down. Now, it is he who stands up and walks over to sit down again in the armchair.

"I too belonged to Disequilibriums."

At that moment, we can hear an ambulance passing on the road. Horns were blasting like mad, I imagine, for cars to move aside to allow the emergency services to pass. I prefer to be down on the street to see the spectacle, not up here in this room. I don't know if I want to continue listening. I feel a mixture of annoyance and curiosity. An unpleasant business with things yet to be discovered. From freak to a man of mystery... Deep down I feel envious. I would have liked to have a secret and then reveal it one day to impress my friends!

Sofia and Erik look frozen. They didn't even bat an eye at Samuel's last statement, either because they aren't surprised or they're so angry that they don't want to reveal their feelings. The problem is that I notice they look more united, more connected to each other. Damn it!

Suddenly there is a huge noise, as if a thunder bolt had struck just above my home. We spring to our feet and rush to the window to see what's happening.

Nothing. The ambulance has already passed. Traffic returns to what it was before. Everything seems normal. Then the noise returns and is louder than ever. It sounds like a machine gun with rays falling one after the other, impacting and breaking things. Like mad people, we rush around the room, not understanding what's happening. I lean out through the open door, but I can't see anything in the rest of the house. Samuel stands under the lintel of the door. Erik grabs me and Sofia, and guides us to stand under the lintel of the door as if to prepare for an earthquake. Sofia looks from side to side, completely disoriented.

Suddenly there was another very loud noise and the room lights up. It's all cloudy outside. So, it can't have come from there. No one has turned on the lights in the living room. When I turn around, I see Sofia, with her mouth agape, pointing at the wall.

In the middle of the very loud noise, we move to stand next to Sofia who is now sitting in the chair looking at the screen where Elsa's image was before. Even Samuel's jaw has dropped open.

"Are you seeing the same thing I am seeing?" We can hear Elsa asking, although we can't see her.

Where Elsa's face had been projected previously on the screen via her webcam, we now see the image of an atomic mushroom, like those they put in documentaries to illustrate what a nuclear explosion is like. The sound continues to be deafening. Sofia grabs my hand and holds it tightly. Good God! I don't understand anything, neither what I am seeing on the wall nor what I am feeling with this contact.

There's no time to answer Elsa because the image changes suddenly. The noise has disappeared. On a black background, we can see large letters in white:

STOP WHAT YOU ARE DOING

If that is surprising, what makes even Sofia stand up violently and release my hand is the sign we are seeing below the letters. We can hear Elsa's voice on the loudspeakers saying:

"Isn't that the sign of infinity, the same kind and colour as the one Samuel has on his videoconferencing profile?"

Samuel moves quickly away from us to go towards the wall and, for the first time since I've known him, I see fear on his face.

CHAPTER 31

Thursday 22 December 2016
Time: 8:30 pm

Sofia

I can't stop thinking about Samuel as we prepare dinner.
The last twenty minutes have been the tensest I've ever
experienced. He has taken off his long overcoat and, without it,
he doesn't look as big as I had thought. He is certainly
muscular, but as always he walks with a slouch and with his
long coat I would never have imagined it. I have to focus
because if not, I'll cut my fingers with this sharp knife.

Cutting carrots on a wooden chopping board isn't difficult,
but doing it quickly as I am accustomed to doing can be risky if
I am not concentrating.

I can't stop thinking about what has just happened. After the
words with the noise appeared and Samuel almost collapsed
with fear, Elsa's image re-appeared on the projection. There
was absolute silence that no one dared to break. David then
stood up and started directing us. He told Elsa to come over
quickly to his house, that he had food in the fridge and that we
would prepare something together. I couldn't stop watching
him as he organised us. I liked how he did it. We needed
someone to take charge of the situation at that moment, and
David took charge. It's not normal for him, and so I'm
impressed. Deep down, I felt very safe next to him.

He normally doesn't take the initiative, but since his
mother's episode, he's different. It served to break the impasse
that has developed, and now between the two of us we start
preparing some *tortillas* and some salads. No one says
anything. It is as if by silent agreement we've decided not to
continue talking until the five of us were all together.

I watch David next to me and I notice that he's accustomed
to being in the kitchen. Erik and Samuel must be setting the

table in the living room. I hope that is what they are doing, instead of arguing. I don't hear anything. So, I suppose that there is peace.

Suddenly, there is a sound of music coming from somewhere in the apartment.

"What's that?" I ask David.

He lifts his head to perk up his ear towards where it is coming from.

"It must be Erik. He saw my brother's *dulzaina* which was in the living room. As he had never seen one before, I showed him how to play it with the main notes."

He falls silent to listen again.

"He plays it quite well."

"Yes, yes," I respond, as I continue what I was doing before. "I asked you about it because I like it."

We continue working in the kitchen, each of us in silence occupied with what we are doing. Through the window, we can see the city, grey after the rain. The black cloud, that cast us in darkness earlier, has faded. I notice the neighbours opposite starting to take in their laundry too late. Suddenly, I notice David is about to break the silence.

"It was nice when you held my hand earlier."

I hear David saying as he stands next to me beating the eggs and looking down at the frying pan with sizzling oil. It's true. At the moment of tension, I grabbed his hand and now I remember that I gripped it tightly. I don't know what it meant for him, but it appears that this comment sounded like what I think it was. Why did I hold his hand? It was an instinctive act, or was it?

"Thank you David," I say the first thing that comes to my head. "I was very tense."

"Any time." He turns to me and smiles.

Oh, oh! It seems that I've just made the conflict worse. David is my friend, every since we were small children, and I have a high regard for him. He's a good guy. It is true that he's grown up a lot and I've to admit that he is quite attractive, but

I've never considered him as anything more than a friend. He's tall, with an athletic body and walks with his own unique style: self-assured and at the same time, with every step he takes he is curious about everything he observes around him. It makes me laugh that he's got a fringe that he keeps brushing away from his face with his hand. He always wears fine, baggy jumpers which look elegant on him. Although his colour combination in trousers is not his strong point, he looks good in them, so much so he attracts glances from the girls in class. Until now, I've always regarded him as a friend, although I have to admit that I've never seen him working in the kitchen and he looks very handsome. However, I'm in a relationship with Erik and I don't want to spoil that.

"Thank you for being my friend," I say, turning to look at him directly.

Suddenly, he leaves the dish and fork on the kitchen counter and, without me doing anything, he moves his face close to mine. He looks at me. I am unable to put down what I'm holding. I look back at him. As in a dance in slow motion, he moves his hands upwards. It feels good. Now, with his hands on either side of my face, he holds my face firmly as his lips touch mine. I don't know what's happening. I feel my world whirling around me. I feel a knot in my stomach, and at the same time, a feeling of peace. I see his mouth opening and I do the same. We kiss fully. The sensation overwhelms me. My heart is pounding a mile a minute. I feel his hands. I like it. With my eyes shut, I can feel nothing but him. What's happening to me?

But something brought me back to reality and, putting down what I have in my hands, I gently remove his hands from my face and stop kissing him. I move away from him. He blushes, lowers his eyes and continues beating the eggs.

"I'm sorry," he says between his teeth, looking down at the dish.

I don't know what to say. My heart has calmed down a little. It felt as if it was going to explode. I've just put myself in a right muddle. Not because Erik might have seen us, since I hear him having a laugh with Samuel in the living room, but because I liked it.

This can't be. David's my childhood friend. This can't happen. I'm going out with Erik.

I think that I've just understood the reason for his strange behaviour in recent weeks. How could I not have seen it before? Would others have noticed it? I am going to put some rationality in this.

"It's nothing," I say in a low voice as I look at the pieces of vegetables I've already cut. "We are under a lot of tension."

He stops beating the eggs and has remained quietly looking at the dish. Then, he turns to look at me for a second. I observe a glint in his eyes, which I've never seen before. He returns to what he was doing before and I finish making the salad in the large dish he's given me.

The doorbell rings loudly.

"Erik, Samuel!" David shouts in the direction of the living room. "Please open for Elsa. I can't at the moment. I've got my hands full."

CHAPTER 32

Thursday 22 December 2016
Time: 10:00 pm

David

So, it seems that Erik has finished telling his story.

I've not been able to look at Sofia throughout the meal. I sat down next to her so that I wouldn't have to do so. Neither did she look at me. I still don't know why the episode in the kitchen happened. I keep asking myself why. If she had slapped me after the kiss, I would feel more at ease, but she didn't.

For me, it was somewhat uncontrollable. Deep down, I think she was right: it's all that tension from before. For a moment, I thought that it could be the end. And here I am, with her sitting next to me. Moreover, she tells me that she is pleased that I am her friend. I thought that it would be the last thing that I would do before the world exploded. And I did it. I've felt quite ashamed of myself since that moment, but she hadn't rejected me in the beginning. I felt her response. I felt it a lot.

"David." I look at Elsa sitting opposite me, moving her right hand from side to side to get my attention. "David, where are you?"

I open my eyes wide. I look first at her and then around the table at the others, ending at Sofia.

"Sorry." I look at Elsa again. "I was lost in my own thoughts."

They all laugh... all except Sofia.

We get up to leave the table. Samuel cleans it with a cleaning cloth and in a matter of seconds, we are again at our laptops and tablets at the table.

I put the situation with Sofia out of my mind. I have to be strong and be serious. We have a difficult problem on our hands, which requires the group to work as a unit.

"I think I owe you all an explanation," Samuel remarks.

"Before you say anything, Samuel," Sofia sits upright and, with her hands crossed, says: "It's clear that someone has hacked into our videoconferencing conversation earlier."

Well, it's true. With all the commotion with the noise, the sentence and Samuel's situation, it hadn't occurred to me that it would be the first conclusion we would reach. I don't know how they did it, but there's someone else out there.

"Has anyone here given our video link details to anyone?" Sofia interrogates us.

Without meaning to do so, we all turn to look at Samuel.

"No, no and no," Samuel responded nervous, feeling under attack. "Stop looking at me. I was here with you and I didn't start the session."

What a cheek! Now the blame is going to fall on Elsa and me. I'm not even bothering to respond to this. It will not change a thing.

"I've always done it," Elsa says, "and I've never had a problem like this."

I get up quickly and in two steps, I reach the Wi-Fi connection router and turn towards them. They're all looking at me. With my right hand, so that they can all see, I pull the switch on the router and all the little lights on the device disappear.

"Now, we have no spies," I say as I sit down again. "Everyone has to connect to the Internet using their own mobile data."

They will probably accuse me of behaving like a jerk, but I don't care. I'm not prepared to be accused in my own home of having spies.

"Someone's observing us," Sofia says again. "This has changed things in the game."

"Of course," Elsa continues, "someone doesn't want us to continue what we've started."

"Well, in my case," says Erik, "they've succeeded in doing the opposite. Now, I'm really interested in continuing." He turns towards Sofia and takes her hand. I can feel my stomach turning. "Before I was interrupted, I wanted to tell you the last message that the Disequilibriums Group received from Sofia's father: 'I am convinced that the real Disequilibrium is coming soon to this city. I am going to travel to fix it. Wish me luck'."

Sofia's face crumbles. I think that we are all coming to the same conclusion.

Erik remains quiet for a moment as he looks down at their clasped hands. For a minute, I think it's a message for me. Sofia does nothing. Erik continues speaking without looking away from their hands.

"After that message, they sent him several, but they received no answer. We don't know anything more." Sofia releases Erik's hand.

At that moment, if there were electricity running through the group when we linked hands with each other, we could have lit a bulb. We look at each other and at Samuel, hair well-groomed again, with whom I am smiling. At this precise moment, we nod and say 'Yes!' to each other. We are united. The thought that someone else is trying to stop us is precisely what is motivating us to carry on.

"I believe that, without saying anything to each other, we've all combined our information and we believe Nicola all the more."

Nobody says anything, but we all nod. Inadvertently, I glance at Sofia and at her lips. I can't forget the kiss. I am distracted just by her presence. But I have to be serious. I cannot put myself in the middle of a couple's relationship, and moreover, they are my friends... if not, I'd be thinking of her everyday.

"Each one has a mission." Erik's voice brings me back to reality. "Remember what Nicola told us: 'Your job is to solve the problem and mine is to watch... the rest I will tell you when you return'. When he said that, I thought that this guy is even crazier than I first thought..." He stops for a moment and then continues, "but now I am convinced that he knows more than he has told us."

I recall that Nicola's words left us astonished that day, but today we remember it. He has become part of the mission. We are ready. We are going to jump. The only thing missing is the music.

"Still," Samuel starts speaking, but waits until we all look at him, "we still have to sort out the music."

What's happening here? Can Samuel read my thoughts? Otherwise, we're all thinking the same thing, but he's the first who dares to mention it.

"According to what he said," Elsa reads from her little note book that she's put on the table, "we have to go to the Eastern Gate and, just as the sun is rising, we have to say the words that he has written. Then we have to go to the intersection of the *Cardus* and the *Decumanus* just as the light of the dawn..."

"At that moment," Erik continues, "if the music to open the portal is played, it will open and we'll be able to enter...."

Like in a chain game, I then take up the story, "From there, our objective is to find the answers and the reasons why the balance has been broken and to try to fix it..."

"Because," Sofia continues and makes us all smile, "according to what he's insisted on again, we cannot fix it with only the information we have at present."

We look at each other again in silence. Outside, in the street, the weather has begun to change. The black clouds from before are releasing all the water they held. The sound of the rain on the window and the cold outside make us enjoy being indoors together.

"OK, Samuel," Sofia makes me jump. "Explain yourself."

Now, he's the centre of attention. As the heating is on high in the apartment, he's rolled up his sleeves and I am drawn to the tattoo on his left forearm near his elbow. I can't quite make it out, but it seems to be a geometric figure. He has noticed me looking at it and lowers his sleeve.

"Approximately a year ago," he starts speaking, as he looks for something on his tablet, "I found something on the Internet which I didn't attach any importance to, but then curiosity got me the better of me."

He stops and looks at Sofia.

"Your father's name appeared."

"Why?" she asks, looking fixedly at him.

Samuel shifts his position on the seat. He leaves his tablet on the table and is rubbing his hands.

"I frequently investigate everyone on the Internet and, when I entered your name, your father's name popped up."

What!!! If I were to speak for everyone in the room, I would say that another bolt exploded on us. This time, it's invisible! This guy was spying on us?

"What?" Elsa asks, with a change in her voice. "Are you saying that you were investigating all of us?"

All eyes are fixed on him, without any pity. All the tension and now all the accumulated anger are now directed at one person. I want to...

"Yes," Samuel continues in a more diplomatic tone of voice. "I normally put the names of people I know on the Internet and follow the trace..." He stops for a moment and looks at all of us. "Have you never done this before?"

Yes, I have to remain quiet as I've done it. I see the others lowering their heads and looking down at the table.

"So," Samuel continues looking up, "I see that I can continue."

We watch him again.

"When I typed in Augustus Canizzaro in the search engine, after several searches, I came across the Disequilibriums. To register, they required more details than normal and one of the requirements was that you have to be of legal age. As always, I completed the form putting in the details necessary to comply with what they had asked."

Outside, it's raining more heavily. Samuel has to speak up because the noise on the window is getting louder.

"Something happened. I don't know if they investigated my IP or if it was some 'electronic contradiction', as I call it when you introduce two different details of your profile from the same IP. But the fact is that they detected an inconsistency. What struck me as strange was that a welcome message appeared... but with limited access."

"What do you mean 'limited access'?" Sofia asks.

"I don't know." Samuel responds. "The only thing that I could see was that people were telling stories about what had occurred in the cities and how they had fixed it." I could never see the messages from the 'organiser' of the group. I knew that it was your father, but the system did not allow me to see anything of his."

"And," Erik intervenes, "How did you know about my parents?"

"That," Samuel scratches his head. "That was outside Disequilibriums." I had put in a series of search alerts on the Internet and, when one of the key words appeared, I would get a message..."

Suddenly he stops. He blushes and, looking at Sofia, he continues:

"When I typed in the Canizzaro name, I began to detect, there were emails for over a year addressed to him, asking him where he was. There were many. But what surprised me was that all of them came from the same IP address in Sweden."

Erik sits upright at the table and stares at Samuel. His sleeves are rolled up and the muscles in his arm are tensing up by the minute. Samuel looks at him and continues:

"And the rest is history. Once Erik joined our class this year, I investigated him on the Internet and, through his surname, I arrived at the IP his parents used in Sweden. This is the last message they sent your father, Sofia."

He turns his tablet round so that we can all see and read:

You are not alone Augustus. We are going to your city to live and we will help you.

CHAPTER 33

Thursday 22 December 2016
Time: 11:00 pm

Sofia

So, my father said goodbye before going away on his trip and never returning!

But where did he really go? How did he disappear?

I'm imagining all kinds of scenarios and it scares me just thinking about them. What if he's still alive?

I want to cry. I want to shout. And by all accounts from what they have said, even my mother is probably aware of everything. And she's hidden it from us her children. I can't believe it. This is worse than any film I've seen up to now, and today I am the main character. For a moment, I want to think that none of this is really happening, that what Erik and Samuel are saying is all rubbish. The fact is that, if only one of them had said it, I would not have believed it. But it cannot be a coincidence that two different people who had never talked about it beforehand should know the same thing.

What am I doing?

Shall I call my mother and tell her? I don't really know what to say to her. I feel deceived. She doesn't have the right to hide it if she really knew about it.

I feel them looking at me. Apart from the story about the Disequilibriums, the group and all the rest, what really eats at me is the thought that my father could be still alive. Everyone is still looking at me. I don't know what to say. I don't know what to do. It's the first time I've felt like this. I am unable to make a decision.

I bury my face in my hands.

I'm sure that they're still looking at me.

I'm going to wake up from this nightmare.

Daddy!' Daddy! but he's not answering.

He's not here.

I'm going to wake up from this nightmare and everything will return to what it was before.

As before? When can I say 'before'? Could it be before my dad disappeared almost a year ago, or half an hour ago?

That's it! I'm not going to be the one to stop this.

Perhaps to lighten up the mood, David picks up his computer and has started to search the Internet. The others follow his lead and we are all again fully immersed in this adventure. Suddenly, I stand up and look at the screen. I cannot help blurting out:

"Sacred Geometry! That's what Elsa was telling us about! The Fibonacci numbers that I found in my father's briefcase. I've just seen how it all works on this webpage. In fact, I've seen reviews in the books I saw in my father's briefcase."

No one is taking notice of me. They are all working on their computers. I prefer it like that. I don't want to be the leader here. No one is asking me anything, which is just as well.

I point out the webpage to each of them and they all see the PHI relationship and how many shapes conform to it. I find a webpage in which they describe some constructions designed using sacred geometry with the application of the *golden number*. Suddenly I stop, look at David and smile.

"Can you lend me a ruler?"

As soon as he brings it to me, I take out the city plan from my bag, on which we had placed the solstice rectangle as Nicola had instructed. I spread it out on a clear area on the table. I notice them observing me, and after measuring a couple of things, doing the calculations and noting them down on a sheet of paper, I show them what I've written.

"I can't believe it!" David exclaims.

"It's the PHI number," Erik says aloud and adds, "the relation between the long and short sides of the solstice rectangle is practically the same as the golden number. It's all sacred geometry."

At that point, I return to the computer and read three pages. Then I lean back on my chair, sigh, look up at the ceiling and say:

"I think I know what my father discovered."

They all stopped looking at their screens and turn to watch me, even Samuel.

"Neither London, Paris nor Bergamo has the same relationship found in Zaragoza. If he was looking for the true city of balance, he found it because that's where he was living."

Erik and David approach and observe the computer screen. At that moment, Erik makes a comment:

"Look! What shocked me most was the little statue with the two faces. I have searched on the Internet, for Greek or Roman gods and found this."

He shows us a photo that's exactly the same as the one we saw at Nicola's house.

"It's the god Janus!" Samuel jumps up and exclaims.

The way he said it, with so much certainty, made us all go quiet, even David who was looking at the maps and checking the measurements of the squares and circles with a ruler. I notice that I no longer regard David in the same way as I did before. Something has changed as of today. It's going to be difficult to treat him in the same way as I've done until now.

Suddenly I felt Erik's hand on mine. At any other time, it would be the most normal thing. In fact, I like it when he does it occasionally. But now, today. What a muddle! No. I have to be self-assured and to show it. If I'm going out with Erik and I like him, I must not conceal anything from him. But that was before I enjoyed the kiss.

"And how do you know this?" Elsa's question to Samuel jolts me from my thoughts.

"I had seen it at some time in a book," he answers as if it was of no importance. "He has two faces because one face looks towards the beginning and the other at the end; one towards birth and the other towards death, towards day and towards night. Therefore, the first month of the year, January, is

214

named after Janus because it represents the face that looks to the start of things."

"It makes sense that Janus is at Nicola's house, as it's at the point of balance." Samuel's conclusion has made me hold him in affection once more.

Erik and I look at each other. He squeezes my hand and smiles. I reciprocate. Everything is becoming more intense because things are squaring up. I read the explanation on the webpage and I become increasingly excited. We have to do the jump, we have to travel back and find the answer.

I'm quiet for a moment and spread out the plan of the city with the tilted solstice rectangle.

"What I've discovered and what you are going to see now is the number of churches there are in Zaragoza. And where are they located? We already know that at the Eastern Gate, there is the Church of La Magdalena, but if we go to the Western Gate, it's next to the Church of San Cayetano. And now you will see it."

I take out another transparency which I had worked on at the weekend. What I did was to draw a square which will include the solstice rectangle. On each of the short sides of the rectangle, I drew a centre line with the same longitude on the long side of the rectangle and, afterwards, I linked the ends of the new lines with other perpendicular lines to form the square. Then, I matched up the ends of this square to the mid-points of the other square so that it would wrap around it and did it like this several times. I was inspired by the symbol we saw at Nicola's house and in my dad's office.

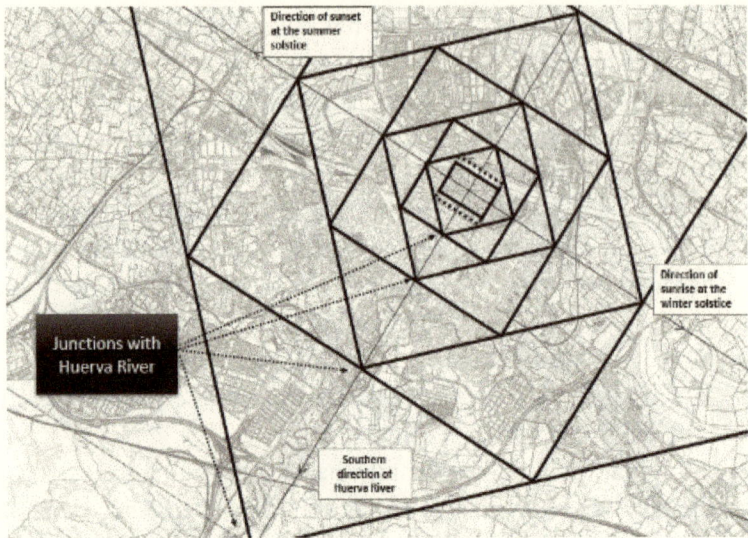

Direction of sunset at the summer solstice

Direction of sunrise at the winter solstice

Junctions with Huerva River

Southern direction of Huerva river

I allow them to observe it for a while and then say:

"If you look, the two lower ends of the first square coincide with the location of the Church of San Miguel and the Church of Santiago."

At that moment, I see the same surprise on their faces as I had on the day I discovered it. I was stunned when I saw it. Drawing the squares, each within the other, was a great discovery for me because the coincidence I saw afterwards was jaw-dropping.

"But there's something else here!" David exclaims and I go closer to the plan to get a better look at the detail.

He stops and also approaches the city plan on the table to get as close as possible to see it.

"How pronounced it is!" He adds. "Since the explanation in class, and considering the four elements of nature and of balance, I had deduced that if Emperor Augustus thought that this was a sacred city, it would be because he discovered the balance of the four elements."

He stops for a moment for a drink of water. I observe every movement he makes with the glass. He's one who gets pleasure when he is having a drink and you can see it from the way he closes his eyes like I do. He does it so smoothly. Today, his fringe gives him an intellectual look, making him more attractive.

But, what am I thinking? I am holding hands with my boyfriend and at the same time looking at another boy in the way I am doing. Sofia, get a grip of yourself! Be true to the decision you have made.

I compose myself.

"The air is clearly identified by the intensity of the wind in the area." I listen to David's explanation. "And the sun, of course. So, it's an area with many hours of light at the end of the year, and the *Cardus* and the *Decumanus* are oriented to find it. The concept of the earth occurred to me when we were in the museum and we read that on the day the city was founded, a priest was pulling a golden plough with two oxen. Specifically, there was a person throwing the earth from the ditch into the inner part of the city to be built. And the water... I had taken it for granted that it was the Ebro River."

At that moment, putting his hand on David's shoulder, smiling broadly, almost comradely, and pointing at the map, Erik says to him:

"You've just discovered and have made us see that the water does not refer to the Ebro River but to the Huerva."

The picture they present is intense, because they look at each other and smile. They look almost like friends and I feel awful. What happened earlier in the kitchen has me turning over inside.

"That's right," he indicates on the map all the points where the vertices criss-cross with the Huerva River to the south.

I have to admit that I had not seen it. It's mind-blowing, I had only noticed the intersection between the streets and the churches, but the intersection with the Huerva River is even more astonishing.

"It's incredible! It's incredible!" Elsa shocks us all with her school-girlish screams.

She can't stop saying it over and over again. We watch her to see if she realises that if she does not calm down, we won't be able to understand what she's saying.

"We have to go and see Nicola right now! It's almost midnight and we've only a few hours to dawn."

"Why are you so sure? Don't you think it's very late to go to someone's house?" I ask her.

Elsa becomes serious.

"I think that we all have an idea of what happened to your father." I feel a lump in my throat, *but this we cannot stop. I am with them. I want to continue.* "Although I don't have proof of everything, This is how I think it was..."

She stands up and, like a teacher, she begins to gesticulate with her arms:

"Emperor Augustus was from a prominent family in Rome and he was sent to Greece to study the classics. He must have acquired an in-depth knowledge of geometry and, specifically, sacred geometry. The truth is that when I told you about the PHI number earlier, it is because when I discovered it, I began to do some more reading on it and I couldn't stop. Everything that is linked to it is fantastic."

She pauses to calm down and then continues,

"I don't know how, but Emperor Augustus discovered what occurred in the location of the original city and established the city of Caesaraugusta, which bore his name, and the construction of the Roman walls show that, in addition to the solstice rectangle, all balance was based on sacred geometry."

At that moment, Erik stands up and intervenes:

"I totally agree. The only thing we need to do now is to sort out the tune to open the portal."

"I think," says Samuel, "that we need a clue and it must be within everything we have in front of us here."

I look at him as he observes the plans on the table. I would like to know what is going through his head. As a chess player, I sometimes think that he's three steps ahead of us. But I agree with him. There is something that does not quite add up. I nod.

"What I can't understand in this whole puzzle is how Janus is connected to all of this," I commented.

There is silence. Instinctively, we pick up our mobiles and without saying anything to each other, we send five text messages from David's house to five different families. It's amusing because Elsa is reading out aloud what she is writing home, which coincides with what I've written to my mother: 'Today we're having a sleepover at David's house to be with him because of what happened to his mother'.

I watch David and I know that he's also sending this message to his Uncle Daniel. I don't know what excuse he's giving. Erik, for sure, is sending one to his mother. He's very close to her.

How I would love to find out who Samuel is sending his message too.

When we finish, hardly saying anything to each other, we pick up our coats and leave. This really is good rapport. What a cool group, as my little brother would say.

Turning around, I see David putting the *dulzaina*, which was in the living room and which Erik was playing before, in his coat.

We all went down into the street, and without saying anything we started walking quickly towards the town centre. It's no longer raining, but the ground is wet and it's very cold. We have to be careful so that we don't slip.

Elsa and I walk a little behind, taking care to put on our scarves and gloves securely. The three boys are walking together ahead of us. Elsa has been quiet for a long time and I realise that she used the excuse of the cold so that we would be together at the back.

She breaks the silence as we walk, "The other day we were talking in the street and you asked me a question."

I don't know what she is talking about, and so I let her continue without interrupting.

"But today, I recognise that I was not completely truthful." She lowers her head as she continues walking.

Without saying anything, I turn towards her so that she can see that I'm listening to her. We are half-way down Paseo Sagasta and, despite the cold, a couple are sitting on one of the benches in the centre, kissing each other. Elsa looks at them for a moment and then continues speaking:

"Today when he took charge after all the commotion with the computer screen, I realised that I can't hide it anymore. Not only was he handsome and a decisive leader, but he also transmitted a feeling of security and courage."

I've only just realised who she is talking about. Oh! I can't say anything to her, just after the boy she is talking about gave me a kiss that I will never forget for as long as I live.

Elsa stops as we reach the department stores, holds my arm and, whispering in my ear so that no one else can hear, she tells me:

"I decided to tell David that I like him and I want to go out with him."

Goodness gracious! What do I say to her now? Everything is whirling around me. As if we didn't have enough on our plate, with all the historical conflict in which we are enmeshed, now I have to contend with one of my best friends wanting to ask the boy who I've just kissed in secret to go out.

"What's the matter, Sofia?" Elsa looks at me very strangely. I must control my expression. "Is there a problem?"

"No, no," I hasten to answer. "Forgive me." This is the only excuse that occurs to me. "With all this trouble with Nicola, I haven't taken it all in at first."

I move away a little. I hold her gently on the arms and smiling at her, I respond:

"I wish you all the very best, Elsa. He's very nice and a good friend. I'm sure it will go very well for you both."

But, suddenly Elsa becomes very quiet and stops smiling.

"The problem is," she hesitates before continuing. "The problem is that I think his heart is already captured by another."

Darn it! I hope she never finds out who she is.

She lifts her gaze, stares at me and says:

220

"But I don't care." With greater determination than normal reflected on her face, she continues speaking, "I am going to tell him, whatever happens."

I can say the only thing that occurs to me:

"Good luck."

She takes my arm and we hurry to catch up with the boys who haven't even noticed that we had stopped. She seems better and even walks with her head held high. The problem is that I suddenly feel a lump in my throat. I can hardly breathe. At this moment, I prefer to focus on my legs moving.

CHAPTER 34

Friday 23 December 2016
Time: 12:05 am

David

There are few people walking at this hour of the night on Don Jaime Street. I see a group of university students going into one of the bars on the adjacent streets. The rubbish men are taking advantage of this hour of the night to collect rubbish with the bin lorry.

I look up at the apartments and there are a few with lights on. Because it's a Thursday night, people go to bed early. Bars, normally overflowing with people from Friday onwards, only have one or two customers tonight.

As we approach Nicola's house, the five of us look at each other and smile because we see a light in his apartment. Although it is hard to press the door bell of a house after midnight, on this occasion Sofia and I outdo each other in order to do it.

Nicola hasn't even asked who it was. I think he's expecting us. We go up the stairs. When we arrive at his apartment, we see that the door is open. We go in immediately. It's clear that he's been waiting for us. He has put out five bowls on the table next to a pot, and is carrying a ladle in his hand. Looking at us as we sit down, he asks us:

"How many spoonfuls of soup do you want?"

The level of complicity between us is impressive. I don't think it would have occurred to us when the History teacher chose us to do this group work. All that we've experienced in such a short time has been so very intense. It's creating bonds of friendship we've never had with others. Elsa sits next to me, puts her arm on my shoulder and smiles at me. She looks at the others and the five of us smile as we put our arms on the shoulders of the person next to us, in a kind of collective hug.

Even Samuel looks excited. I'm going to remember this moment for a long time.

Without waiting for our answer, Nicola begins to fill the bowls with soup in which I can see pieces of vegetables and meat. This is not the time to say that I don't like soup. Of course not.

"It's cold today," Nicola says as he fills the bowls.

And he's right. With all this problem, none of us realise that we've not had any dinner, and as I see the food, I'm filled with an incredible pang of hunger. I taste it carefully because it's still releasing steam. The first sip is like a delicacy from the gods. But if I hate soup... It is not salty or tasteless; it's just right. I have to change my taste for this dish. The meat is chicken. It's delicious. I like the food and today, I like the place. The apartment is the same as we saw it on the last occasion we were here, everything in white, with the same decor.

Suddenly, the five of us observe the statuette at the entrance now that we know what it is - the head of the god Janus. We all look at each other and wink as we eat the soup.

"I have to admit that I expected you a little earlier," Nicola starts saying. "If you are going to do what you have to do," he stops for a moment to look at Erik's wristwatch, "you don't have a lot of time."

There's absolute silence after he speaks. It's Sofia who takes the initiative. Before speaking, she gathers her hair to one side. I can't take my eyes off her pretty neck. I can't stop thinking about the kiss. I can't be distracted! I have to focus on the present!

"You have convinced us. We will do it."

"No," Nicola replies. "It is *you* who have convinced yourselves." And then he adds, "Isn't that so?"

As time is flying, we tell him up to where we've reached and all the information we have, including what Erik's parents and Sofia's father had said and done. I would be speaking for everyone if I said aloud that we no longer think that this story is rubbish, even Erik himself is one of the most involved. He is excited as he looks at Nicola directly in his eyes. We are bursting with excitement, but we know there's something missing. And the old man has recognised it.

We finish telling him all that we know and fall silent. He looks at us. His blue eyes convey serenity and, at the same time, assurance. Today, he's not wearing anything on his head. His shoulder-length hair is completely white, which gives him an even more extraordinary appearance at this time.

After clearing and cleaning the table, we notice that he's left the room and, a few seconds later, he returns with a paper. It doesn't look like normal paper, but rather a very old piece of paper. In terms of modern sizes, we could say that it is an A2 sheet. As he spreads it on the table, we see that it is a very old parchment paper. Although it is very blurred, I can still make out some Roman letters within a rectangle. There are two columns and something I recognise but can't see very clearly as it is very blurred. Suddenly, I recognise it and blurt out aloud,

"It's the inscription of the ashlar found in the Eastern Gate!"

We approach the parchment to study it more closely as Nicola moves backwards in the room. Without being able to touch it, we study it several times. Sofia and Elsa take out some papers from their backpacks and try to note down what is written on it.

The column on the left is the same as we have seen on the ashlar that we have studied in recent days. The column on the right is totally new to me, because that is the part that has always appeared to be damaged and illegible.

As we are all sitting at the table studying the parchment, no one speaks, including Samuel who has abandoned his tablet and is totally engrossed by this new piece of evidence. On this occasion, compared to other times when we were in this apartment, there is nothing outside to break the silence of the night. It seems that everything around us is preparing us for the following step.

I am able to put the letters together, and together we correct it until in the end, we agree on what is written:

PARVUM EST MAGNO UT MAGNUM OMNIBUS EST.

As we read it again and again, Nicola sits with us around the table and we all look at him.

"According to legend, when Emperor Augustus finished the city, he insisted that the builders left a clue in the Eastern Gate for coming generations. And this he did on the ashlar. From what you have told me, you have gathered enough information in recent days."

My blood is boiling. My hands are sweating. I see that I am not the only one who is extremely nervous by what I'm hearing. This is completely new and it's taking us to a place that I don't know if we are prepared to go. I try to look for something outside to distract me. There's nothing. Silence continues to be our companion tonight.

"He was very proud, because he himself used it to return to Rome," Nicola continues his commentary. "No one knows how but, through his sacred city, he had created a transport through space." He looks at us in silence, and then continues, "And through time, without realising it."

As incredible as this sounds, this part of the story seems too far-fetched for me, although it doesn't cease to amaze me every time I think of it.

"He felt that he deserved it for all he had done for Rome, and as he knew the secret of how to use it, he saw no problem in using it," he continues. "He was capable of going and coming, always with the intersection of the *Cardus* and the *Decumanus* being the point of entry and exit."

He stops for a moment to take air. Today, he looks tired.

"But a problem emerged. Some soldiers from the Twins Tenth Legion (*Legio Decima Gemina*) discovered the secret the emperor had used and gradually it became complicated because they began to use it differently from the emperor. This legion

225

had accompanied him on his campaigns in the north of Italy, France and Britain."

He stops a moment as if trying to remember what he's going to say next.

"Emperor Augustus found out and the first thing he did was to forbid its use. And in a fit of anger, he himself took a hammer and chisel, and completely destroyed the column of letters on the right."

Samuel looks almost like a madman, wide-eyed and mouth agape. Nicola had us completely engrossed in the story. With his hands, he simulated the action of hitting something with a hammer. My hands are wet with sweat and I am fidgeting on my seat. I need him to continue. I want to know the whole story. I want him to continue telling it to us as he's doing now.

"He started to knock out the letters on the left column, but just as he was doing so, the city came under attack from outside the walls and he had to organise its defence. Everything got very complicated. He had to continue his conquest of other countries, and he never remembered to finish the destruction he had started."

My hands are no longer sweating. I simply do not feel them, as I don't feel the rest of my body. The expressions on my friends' faces show the same intensity of surprise and fear that must be reflected in mine. Sofia breaks the silence:

"But how is it that you have the inscription on this document?"

Nicola looks at her and patiently answers:

"When they had finished building the Eastern Gate, and specifically this ashlar, Emperor Augustus had created the post of watchman for this *Cardus* and *Decumanus*, the 'Watchman of Balance' as he called it." As he said that, he pointed through the window at the intersection of the streets. "He knew that the sacred city would last for many years if the basic principles on which the city was designed were maintained."

Samuel is touching his head. His hair is no longer as well groomed as it was when he came to my house. He is back to his normal appearance. He is looking at the photo of the ashlar on his tablet. He says nothing.

"The first watchman did something that Emperor Augustus did not know about, and would never have authorised it. After the inscription was carved on the ashlar, the watchman used a parchment he found, put it on the wall of the ashlar and passed a charcoal stick several times over it to copy the inscription. The watchman hid the parchment in the city itself and communicated its location to every watchman who succeeded him."

We couldn't be more silent than we are now. As if I could will his lips to move with a look, I watch him intensely to make him continue speaking.

"I am the first watchman who has had to collect the parchment from its hiding place and to show it to someone else."

We say not a word. The silence in this room is as intense as on the street.

I wonder if we are the only ones he has shown.

CHAPTER 35

Friday 23 December 2016
Time: 12:55 am

Sofia

His last sentence prompted me to ask him what I wanted to know since I saw the parchment.

"What does the column on the right mean?"

"I am only the Watchmen of Balance and if that balance is in danger," Nicola explains, making us listen to him very closely because he said the key word, "... I can only help others re-establish it, but I can never do it myself. You have compiled a lot of information. Some of it is important in order to start the journey and the rest you will need later. Only *you* can decide when and how."

This leads to another moment of silence. Then, he stands up and stares at the figurine on the table next to the entrance.

"When you return, I will help you combine all the information you find."

"It is almost one o'clock in the morning," David starts saying, "and without dictionaries, we can't translate it."

Nicola is silent and then continues,

"I will tell you the meaning, but the rest you will have to find out yourselves."

He pauses for a moment and adds,

"The exact translation from Latin is:

THE SMALL IS TO THE LONG, AS THE LONG IS TO THE
WHOLE.

Now I am going retire for bed because I have to be awake before dawn. I am beginning to feel my age. You can stay here for as long as you want, if that helps you to prepare for the jump."

I have to admit that I am as confused as the others. How can he go? He can't. We have to make the jump in a few hours and he has not told us anything. It is true that he has shown us something that we were not expecting and that it's very important in all this business. I wonder how much historians would give to have the parchment he has just shown us. In any case, the sentence does not say anything and it is assumed that there is the clue.

As he is walking away, I say to him, "Nicola, please don't go yet. We don't know what to do with this."

There's a moment of silence, and then replies,

"I trust you, and I am sure that you will know how to find the way. I will be awake before you have to go."

And he leaves, plain and simple, without giving any more explanations. I turn around and look at the others. They look back at me and shrug their shoulders, and then we return to the parchment. We have no other option but to verify the response.

I hear a message alert on my mobile. As I lift the screen, I see that it's a message from my mother. I had completely forgotten about her. I think that I haven't behaved well. I would have to go back home and tell her everything that they have told me in the last few hours and in the end to ask her directly about my dad. I don't know how she would react, nor I for that matter. I suppose that it wouldn't really matter what she tells me because, whatever happens, it would be difficult to believe her, although deep down, I think she knows everything. I imagine that she will be angry with me and would not dare tell me on the phone what she thinks, but may prefer to tell me in a simple message. I don't think I'm going to like it.

Opening and reading the message, I have a sinking feeling, and I feel very guilty. Not only does she not show anger, but that she understands that we would want to be with David at this difficult time. At first, I thought she had a double intention, but now I see that it's not so. In the end, my mother always tries to make things good between us. I feel more relaxed. With a smiley face, I send back a message in reply, 'I love you. Thank you'.

"That's it!" Elsa jolts me from my thoughts. "How did it take me so long to realise it?"

We watch her in surprise and once again she writes the translation that Nicola gave us on a sheet of paper. She studies the words. Suddenly, she relaxes. We are looking at her in total seriousness. Now is not a time for jokes. I hope she has really found out something. Her expression changes and she smiles at us all. Pointing to the translation, she says:

"It refers to the golden number." She recognises that we don't understand what she is talking about. So she explains, "This is sacred geometry. Do you remember what I said about the PHI number? Well, this refers to it. The golden ratio establishes that the small is to the long, as the long is to the whole."

On the screen on his tablet, Samuel shows us a photo of the drawing that Elsa had done the first time she explained it to us.

"Normally, it is applied to the ratio between segments. As I have explained, this geometrical ratio has been venerated by all world cultures. We can find it in art, musical composition, even in the proportions of our own bodies and, in general, throughout nature, 'hidden' behind the Fibonacci sequence."

She falls silent, looking at the parchment. Then, in a deep voice, she continues:

"The golden ratio is a unique way of dividing a unit into two parts in geometrical progression."

She looks at Samuel and smiles as he looks at what she explained to us the last time on his tablet.

"This clearly demonstrates my theory about Emperor Augustus: he based everything on sacred geometry," She finishes her explanation.

Elsa looks proud of what she has discovered, and I would be lying if I didn't say that we are very happy that she's with us. Instinctively, David puts his hand on her right shoulder to congratulate her and she turns quickly towards him and with very wide eyes, smiles back at him. David is not aware of anything. That small innocent gesture is going to have consequences.

I focus again on what we are doing. We have before us a hidden message on a stone that the Romans used to construct the old city, for which a historian would give millions. But personally, I have no idea what our next step is going to be.

"And how is this going to help us now, Elsa," I can't help asking.

There's silence. Neither she nor the boys say anything. It has been a real discovery, but we don't yet know how to use it.

CHAPTER 36

Friday 23 December 2016
Time: 1:30 am

David

I can't stand it! No one is making a decision. We have a pile of information on the table and we don't know what to do. After the most important days of our lives, we have arrived at a special point. How I have changed. As a person who has always waited for all the information before deciding, I am the one who is now put out if we don't make a decision quickly. Sofia must have infected me.

I get up and pace around the table a couple of times. Everyone asks me if I am OK. I continue pacing. Suddenly, Sofia grabs my arm and says,

"Stop, you are making us nervous. What are you doing?"

"I am pacing around," I respond.

"And what rubbish is this?" Erik asks.

"I'm doing the same as you. The only difference is that you are all seated around the table and with a lot of information in front of you: going around in circles." I retort and I get my own way. I have broken the impasse.

Elsa can't stop looking at me and smiling. What I have done must have seemed friendly to her. I sit down between her and Sofia. I carefully open the parchment Nicola has given us and put a blank sheet of paper in the middle of the table so that we can all see.

I start drawing as I speak:

"Let's see. We have on one side a stone which was in the Eastern Gate," and I draw on the middle of the page a small rectangle, "which has two parts, one with an inscription we can understand." I draw a vertical line dividing the rectangle into two equal parts. "We know that on one side of the rectangle, used to 'travel' back to Rome, it has something to do with the god Janus." I draw two lines from the left side of the rectangle to the top where at one end, I put JUMP TO ROME and at the other end JANUS.

I look at the faces of the rest of the group. Something has changed. On my right, Elsa and Samuel, next to her and then Erik and Sofia on my left, they are all following my drawing and thinking at the same time. Sofia looks at me differently. She has released Erik's hand.

I take advantage of the moment and continue speaking:

"In addition, there is the relationship with the golden number." I draw a line from the right side of the small rectangle to the right side of the paper and at the end of it, I put the PHI. "On the other side, we have the design of the city with the tilted solstice rectangle," and I draw only in the central area below, "which we have said is linked to the four elements of nature," I put a small circle in the half of each side of the solstice rectangle, "with the fifth element in ether in the centre."

I am going to draw another circle in the centre so that it is clear.

Guessing what I was about to do, Elsa puts her left hand on my right arm and interrupts me, "Wait, don't do a circle..."

We all look at her. Internally, I try to anticipate what she is going to say, but she forestalls me.

"... at the intersection, there is an eight-pointed star."

We had seen this small figure at the beginning, but we hadn't mentioned it.

"The eight-pointed star, the polygon of eight sides, the octagon is..." Samuel jumps to his feet and startles us all. "It's..."

He is pacing around the table too. He looks like a kid. He walks and laughs. He looks at us and laughs again. This guy sure has a problem! Suddenly, he stops again and, looking at us as he has never done before, he asks:

"Don't you see it?"

We are absolutely nonplussed as if struck down in a boxing match. He's left us on the ground. From our expressions, I can see that none of us is following what he is saying. We must be light years away from his mind.

It's almost funny because he keeps running his hands through his hair. As Nicola has the heating turned down low, he hasn't taken off his long coat. So he presents a rather jokey picture.

At last he deigns to enlighten us. Although I suspect that it's the killer look that Sofia threw him that may have more to do with getting him to calm him.

"Balance!"

He looks at us all with his eyes fully open and his eyebrows raised high. For the second time, I must admit that I feel even more lost.

"Balance!" At last, he sits down and continues speaking more calmly. "The number eight in ancient times was linked to equity, with balance."

He gives us a few seconds to get even more impressed. I get up and then go back to my chair. I don't know how I feel, but I can't shake off the feeling that I've been in a dream for several days.

"It comes from Ancient Greece, from Pythagoras. I don't remember the whole story at the moment, but what I *do* remember is that the number eight is a number of great power. It was called the Universal Harmony and was linked to the celestial octave, to love, friendship, prudence and inventiveness."

Then, he becomes serious, looks out the window and continues:

"What is true is that the first moment I began to think about this was when we were in the Plaza San Felipe and were walking on the octagon at the base of the old tower. I remember noting down a large number eight in my notepad."

He looks at our faces. I don't know what he's looking for or what he has discovered in our eyes because mine are like a well which keeps filling up with absolutely incredible information.

"And how do you know all of this?" Elsa asks him very gently.

"From Disequilibriums," he answers looking at her. At last, he stopped passing his hand through his hair. "As I told you before, I managed to get onto their online forum for a time."

He sits down. He leans back on his chair as if he had just discovered the moon and was telling us about it for the first time.

"One of the members said it and of all the content shared on the forum, it received the most 'likes' while I was active."

We continue looking at him in silence.

"It is true that the symbol has eight points. It is not exactly an octagon even though it's made up of two tilted squares," Sofia says as she looks at the drawing I've done. It is clear that we have all seen it in many places in the city, in the old buildings and paintings.

Startled by the sound of snoring, we look at each other and smile.

"How is this guy able to sleep with all the noise we are making?" Erik remarks.

We look again at the material scattered on the table, moving around slowly so as not to wake him up. I finish drawing the two small tilted squares, emphasising the outlines of everything.

"OK," I continue, as if the interruption by Samuel had not taken place because I don't know if it changes what we are doing, apart from the idea of balance of course. "On the other hand, we have the symbols." I draw the circle around the tilted solstice rectangle like the one we see in Nicola's house.

I look around Nicola's house and start drawing again, but this time in silence. Around the word JANUS, I draw a head quickly to represent the god's head.

At that moment, Sofia picks up a pencil and in total silence writes 'MY FATHER'. I suppose it's not going too well. It must all be very difficult for her. I'm not surprised that she has written it next to the words 'JUMP TO ROME' which I had written earlier. I'm no longer haunted by the memory of the kiss in the kitchen as often as I was. At last, I am managing to focus on what we're doing. She's very pretty, but sad at the same time. However, I'm her friend and I must help her.

"Thank you, Sofia," I say to encourage her, making an effort to smile. She looks at me and returns the smile, although not with her usual happy expression.

Erik now picks up the pencil and on the right, in a completely isolated area, he writes 'TUNE FOR JUMP'. I add 'EMPEROR AUGUSTUS' under the tilted solstice rectangle. Thereupon, Erik writes 'SACRED CITY' under what I've written.

Samuel picks up the pencil, approaches the centre of the paper and stops. He looks at the drawing that we have done and putting the pencil back down, he stands back. I don't know if he has written what he was thinking about because he wasn't sure or because he thought that we won't understand. I look at him, but he has already moved away to search for something on his tablet.

We stand in silence looking at what we've drawn. Slowly, we begin to draw lines to link up parts of the drawing with others. Elsa links the PHI to the solstice rectangle.

We link all the parts we have put down on the paper. I look at the paper again. I see that the 'TUNE FOR JUMP' is alone, without a link to anything else. But something seems to be missing on this drawing.

Suddenly, Sofia picks up the pencil and writes the word 'UNBALANCED'. First, she puts it above the solstice rectangle. Then, she erases it. She has doubts. I think that she doesn't know where to put it. I can't help her either, because there at the bottom is the basis of all of this, and perhaps the opposite: 'BALANCE'. But the consequence we've been observing is that people are losing their balance and I can't help remembering my mother. I should be with her if she wakes up. I'm a bad son. No! I have to stop blaming myself. I know that I cannot be there. So, when I manage to calm down, I take the pencil carefully from Sofia's hand (not without touching her a little). As I write, I say aloud:

"I am sure that, in the era of Augustus, they wrote in another way." I write the word 'DISEQUILIBRIUMS' at the bottom of the sheet.

I look at the others and I see that they all agree. We look at the sheet again. I like it all, apart from leaving the 'TUNE' all alone. I check to see that we are all looking at it, but we still can't make the first step.

"Elsa," I break the silence, "what is the PHI number?"

"I don't know it offhand..." She remains quiet for a moment. Then she says, "but we could calculate it."

Quickly, she picks up the pencil and begins to write the numbers of the Fibonacci sequence which she had explained before from top to bottom: 1, 2, 3, 5, 8, 13... and so, by always adding the two last numbers to calculate the following, she puts the last number to the right of each number, the division sign between both and begins to divide the first numbers.

I realise what she's doing. So, I continue the Fibonacci sequence below and put the last number at the side. When I get tired, I choose a division and start to do it on the side. Erik and Sofia have each taken one and are also doing divisions. Samuel also does it on his tablet. Doing divisions at 2 o'clock in the morning is not the most exciting thing for a 16 year old, but I glance at the others and we are all absolutely focused on what we are doing.

After some time, we all put down our pencils, and we look at the different divisions. I start to put down numbers until they agree:

1.6180339887498948420458683...

"I think we've got you!" I exclaim, looking at the paper and indicating the number with the pencil.

"Well yes," Samuel responds with his marked local accent as he shows us the same number on his tablet screen. "You have been as quick as the programme I have here. Congratulations!"

He makes us smile, but we're too tired to lose our focus. We feel proud of ourselves. For a while, I have this same feeling of friendship again, which is as strong as I've felt it before. Working with them, being so united is creating an incredible feeling of closeness.

But after five minutes of silence, no one says or does anything. It seems that we are stuck again. I think we are getting used to it and, deep down, I know that, in the end, it will all work out. Suddenly, Erik picks up the pencil and draws a line on the drawing linking the 'PHI' to the 'TUNE FOR THE JUMP'. We are silent and we hear him beginning to whistle. I don't understand anything. I don't know what he's doing. What I do know, however, is that Erik has music in his blood and will be able to combine anything with music.

"Erik needs an instrument," Sofia says aloud.

What a very strange idea! In any case, in a few hours we need to find the tune that Nicola told us about in order to do the jump. I observe him and also Sofia, and I notice that she is looking at me strangely. I put on a face to say I don't understand and then, she suddenly elbows me in the side.

But, it was not the nudge from her arm that made me realise what she wanted to tell me, but the impact of the dulzaina I'm carrying in my pocket on this side of my ribs.

"Here, take it," I say to Erik, with a smile, as I take out the instrument and hand it to him.

They must be asking themselves what I'm doing with a *dulzaina* in the early hours of Friday morning. Now I remember that when we were leaving my house I realised that we had to get ready to make the jump and that Nicola had told us about the music. It was a reflex action when I saw my brother's *dulzaina* from school. So, let's see what Erik can do.

On a sheet of paper, Erik writes numbers from one to seven on a sheet of paper and, next to it, in a second column, he writes musical notes starting from C. When he reaches number eight, he stops.

1   C

2	D
3	E
4	F
5	G
6	A
7	B
8	

Why had it not occurred to me before?

"What is happening, Erik?" I ask him.

I can't disguise my anxiety at his discovery and how he suddenly seems to be stuck. I would continue to write the sequence.

"We are taking the scale of C Major," without taking his eyes from what he has written as if trying to continue his internal deduction, "because it is the most widely used in Western music." He speaks like an expert. "We will therefore exclude the black piano notes, and use C as the tonic note. That leaves us with C, D, E, F, G, A, and B, without sharps or flats. So 7 notes, but our code is based on 10: 9 numbers plus zero."

Samuel stretches his arms over the paper and makes little drawings with his fingers on the numbers. Then, suddenly to everyone's surprise, he bends forward and buries his head between his arms. Sofia looks at me and frowns. Elsa is nervous. She looks at Erik and at me, not knowing what to do.

Samuel continues to be silent with his head still buried in his arms.

"But..." Erik says without looking away from the paper. He scratches his head and continues speaking, "At this point, we have to resolve the problem of having a scale based on 7 while our code is based on 10." He looks in Samuel's direction as if seeking his approval. "Our first code ends in 8. Precisely 8."

"THE NUMBER OF INFINITY!" Samuel shouts out, without raising his head.

Now they have lost me! I hope they explain it because I am beginning to feel cold and sleepy at the same time. With a such a long delay, I'm not sure we are going to succeed.

"Don't you see?" Samuel stands up and points at what Erik has written.

No one is smiling. I think that it is the second time tonight that he has taken us for fools, although I have to admit that he amazed us before.

"When Erik reached 8 on the scale he was doing," he explained, "I saw it and I suppose he did too, and that's why he stopped."

He stops and stares at our Swedish friend. Elsa is totally impressed. She is also staring at Erik.

"8 is the only number in a scale of 8 with two interpretations," Erik explains. "8 refers to C again, so that it takes us back to the same note, but at an octave higher. This establishes an infinite loop... So 9 would be D and if our system were not decimal, we would continue like this *ad infinitum* always going back to 8, in the first instance, in a clearly defined loop."

Sofia is silent. She looks at all of us. I think she doesn't know what to do. Her ability to make decisions, as she has always done before, seems to have abandoned her. This problem, together with the disappearance of her father, has changed her.

My mind keeps going round and round in circles. The symbol of infinity! How is it possible? Is this all a coincidence? The symbol that Samuel has on his profile, it's the same one that appeared on the projection at my home when they blocked our conversation. And furthermore, it is linked to the octagon, as a symbol of balance, and to the 8-pointed star.

No one is speaking. We are all looking at the numbers.

"Very well," I say, hitting the table. "So we have the '8', the symbol of infinity. So, what is it for? How do we continue the music? I have no idea," I fix my eyes on Erik who is gazing at me with an almost distant look.

He has all the pressure on his shoulders at this moment, because even Samuel is looking at him too.

"OK," Erik starts again, sitting up straight on the chair and taking up the paper and the pen again. "I am going to consider the '0' as a 'silence'." He is serious and very focused. At last, he takes command of the situation and says, "So, our first sequence 1618 would be C, A, C, Top C (an octave higher)."

Now he substitutes the PHI number with musical notes.

1=C; 6=A; 1=C; 8=Top C; 0=SILENCE

Erik begins to play the music, stops, starts again and, after a few seconds, is playing a tune based on the first five digits of the PHI number.

CHAPTER 37

Friday 23 December 2016
Time: minutes between dawn

Sofia

It's still night, yet we can see the first light of dawn. The door of the Church of La Magdalena is still in darkness. The building is lit up at the beginning of nightfall to provide touristic views of the city and it is switched off in the middle of the night to save electricity. So the only light in the plaza is from the few street lights in the area. We are alone in the street. The bars nearby are still closed. All is peaceful and still, except us.

I'm absolutely terrified. I remember last night when, after listening several times to the tune Erik was playing on the dulzaina, we heard Nicola's deep voice from inside his room saying:

"Get a rest, tomorrow is going to be a hard day. You have already found what you are looking for."

We were startled. We thought that he was sound asleep.

I then mentioned to the others that I thought he also said he knew that we would find it. But nobody else heard it. After that, our faces lit up and we went to sleep as best as we could in the living room. We arranged ourselves between the large sofas and the rug on the floor, and despite being very afraid, I fell asleep almost immediately. Fortunately, Nicola had left some blankets because, if not, we would have been frozen. How cold it was in his apartment!

It was Nicola himself who woke us up a few hours later with the smell of coffee and by switching on the lights.

"Good morning," he greeted us with great kindness. "I don't know if at your age you drink coffee, but if you have not already, after the night you've had and what awaits you today, I suggest you drink it."

In my case, he was right because it was the first time that I had ever drunk coffee. In any case, the greatest surprise was when we went into the bathroom we found five bags, each equipped with a toothbrush, toothpaste, soap and a towel. How could he have known that we were going to spend the night in his home? Every minute seemed more unsettling.

During breakfast, we went over everything we were going to do. He reminded us that we could not carry anything from the present to the 'other side' (as he referred to it). So in the same bag that he gave each of us, we put everything we had. I packed my whole backpack in which I keep everything that I carry around everywhere with me.

None of us wanted to ask the key question, but I imagine that we were all wondering what we were going to do there and, more specifically, how we were going to return. The first day he explained it to us, he enumerated exactly the steps we had to follow, although on that day, I thought that I was immersed deep within the madness of a disturbed person. Today, I remember his words so clearly. We have already put so much trust in this man to stop now when the decision to make the jump had already been taken. But, what's the purpose of all of this? I deliberately ask myself this question constantly in order not to forget that everything I'm doing has an explanation and makes sense. Otherwise, I imagine that I would truly go mad or simply, would not do it.

While we were organising ourselves, Elsa took me aside and, in a low voice, said:

"I'm going to tell him soon. I want to do it before the jump."

I stood there simply looking at her, not knowing what to say. I was surprised to see that there was someone in the group who was more interested in something else other than the 'jump'. Well, love is love. At this moment, I wasn't going to allow myself to be distracted from what we were about to do, but I nodded and smiled, just before Samuel asked me if I was going to eat the croissant that was left over at breakfast.

243

I noticed that Elsa tried to keep as close to David as she could, and I wondered whether he was aware of what was happening. From his expression, he appeared to be more naive that I had thought.

When we were ready to leave his home, Nicola stopped us for a moment, wished us luck and told us precisely what I had been thinking about a few seconds earlier.

"Don't ever forget why you are doing this," he said gravely.

Then, he handed each of us a small figurine which fitted in our trouser pocket. It was a small replica of the head, or rather, the head with the two faces of the god Janus. As he gave it to us, he told us:

"I don't expect you to have any problems. But, if something happens, this will be your last resort. Show this figurine." He stopped for a moment and then continued, "And say that the Watchman of Balance gave it to you."

He was quiet for a moment and, putting his hands together, he closed his eyes. He seemed to be praying and of course, no one interrupted him. Then, he opened his eyes and gave us each a kiss on the forehead. Suddenly, he remembered that he needed to say something.

"I almost forgot," he said, as he looked at each of us seriously, "Never draw the DISEQUILIBRIUMS sign in front of anyone."

"Why?" David asked him immediately.

"Remember you are going to try to re-establish balance by travelling there where it was all designed." He fell silent, turned his head to look at the statuette of Janus on the table at the entrance. Why would he be looking at it? I remember wondering about it at that moment. "It's the only thing you need to know."

With that response, no one said anything more. So, we headed for the door to leave. But at that moment, I could stand it no more. I turned towards him. Erik was holding the door open, but seeing that I had turned around, he closed the door again. Elsa, David and Samuel were already going down the stairs.

"Do you know anything about my father?" I asked him directly.

The reaction I saw on his face worried me. It was a mixture of seriousness, surprise and something else that I could not identify. His expression reminded me very much of the expression on the face of the guide at the museum when I asked her last week why the *Cardus* and *Decumanus* in the city were tilted. Then he relaxed, approached me and took my right hand in his hands. He put his fingers on mine as if to press them a little until he stopped on the ring on my middle finger.

"Who gave you this ring?"

I could not believe he was asking this question. Is it possible that he was asking me something that he already knew the answer for?

"My father," I answered.

"May it always remind you of him," he responded, releasing my fingers.

"But do you know where he is?" I asked again and I think I must have looked anxious.

He was quiet for a moment and then he looked at me with tenderness.

"Isn't he with you?" He said, looking down at my ring.

"No," I answered.

"Then, I suggest that you focus on those who *are* with you," he remarked and bade me farewell with his hands.

From the time we left his house to the time we arrive at the Plaza de la Magdalena, I have been thinking about his last words. I suppose he's right and that's when I begin to feel guilty for not being kinder to my mother and not going back to talk to her. Suddenly, David shouts:

"Look! It's starting! There's very little time left!"

CHAPTER 38

Friday 23 December 2016
Time: one minute between dawn

David

My heart is beating at such an incredible rate. Deep down, I'm trembling with what I am feeling within me. This is the most fantastic experience I've ever had in my life. I'm very happy that I'm involved in this adventure. We're going to re-establish balance! Although I ought to have more humility and be more thoughtful than simply thinking that we're going to try to re-establish balance!

During the walk to the church, I've been watching my companions. Although I continue to feel the same way towards Sofia, I now see Erik in a different light. I've discovered a great person. With a lot of cool perseverance, he has succeeded in discovering the last clue we needed. I'm very proud to be part of this team that the five of us have formed.

This is my last thought when I look up. At the top of the church, the sun is beginning to light up the tower and I shout at the others to look up. I can't stop looking up, knowing that behind the facade in the roof, there is a little gate built with bricks. Since the day Sofia saw it, we still haven't found out why it is there.

Suddenly, I feel Elsa grab my arm and is making a sign for me to stop a moment. I don't understand what the problem is. We are super tense at the moment and so I move away from the group. What's the matter with her? I notice Sofia looking at me as I turn to Elsa. We move four paces away from the rest of the group towards the benches in the plaza.

"David, I want to have a word with you."

It's a little strange. We ought to be with the others, preparing for what we have to do. As the first light of dawn can be seen in the sky, against her dark skin, the white of her eyes and teeth shine like lights in the darkness. Her look is insistent and I notice a tension between happiness and deep anxiety. She keeps rubbing her hands, and standing next to me, her eyes are level with mine.

"Elsa," I respond nervously as I glance at the others. "We have to hurry. We have to leave now."

"But..." she starts doubtfully, "there's something important that I must tell you."

Her intention continues to be a mystery to me, but now it's not the best time.

"Elsa, now is not the time."

She jumps quickly, "Then, when?" She looks down at her hands. "What I have to say is very important to me."

I put my hands on her arms and, with the best smile I could manage, I say to her:

"I promise you that after the jump, we'll talk in private."

She looks back at me with expressionless eyes.

"I promise you!" I insist. "I swear. But now, let's go please."

"OK!" Her face lights up with happiness again. "As soon as we do the jump, OK?"

I nod. I give her my hand in a gesture of agreement, and without releasing her hand, I turn and we join the rest. Sofia frowns as she sees our linked hands. I release Elsa's hand immediately. I don't know what she's thinking. Now, we cannot be distracted from the jump.

"Let's go! Let's go!" I say, clapping my hands hard to take command of the situation again.

Like robots because we have instructions on what we have to do, we go towards the wall on which the old Eastern Gate is drawn. The five of us hold hands, and looking at the painted inscription, we read aloud what is written:

PORTA ROMANA QUI FACIUN(T) TE LA(RES) RECEDANT

I had learnt it by heart, but when we got there, with all the nervousness, I had completely forgotten it. Fortunately, it was written on the wall, and that enabled me to recite it. "Roman gate, let those who built you return to your country," I repeat to myself. I hope it works.

Anyone in Plaza de la Magdalena at this time would see five young people shouting some words, and then suddenly running at full speed towards Calle Mayor. He would think that we were mad, and it would be no wonder.

We notice behind us that the sun is coming out. It is beginning to light up the top of the buildings. The sunlight continues downwards. We are running at full speed. Elsa is first and she demonstrates her physical prowess. Samuel is last. Barely able to keep up, he manages to pick up the pace with the rest of the group.

We've spoken several times about having to be very careful when we reach the intersection with St Vincent de Paul Street. So, when we reach the traffic lights, despite not wanting to, the four of us suddenly come to a halt. The cars keep coming. We almost bump into each other. We wait for Samuel. Just then, the pedestrian light turns red. Several cars and a bus are coming. We wait.

"Oh, goodness! We're not going to get there on time," Sofia says, looking back and pointing at sunlight moving downwards on the building.

When at last the light turns green for us to cross and, checking first to see that no one was coming unexpectedly, we run across the street. At full speed, we rush up Calle Mayor. Samuel, apparently spurred on by Sofia's words, is now in second place behind Elsa.

"Quickly!" I shout behind me, when I turn and see Sofia lagging a little behind.

It starts getting very tense. The sunlight is moving down. It will soon light up the intersection and, if we don't arrive on time, we will miss our chance. Suddenly, I hear a scream:

"Ay!"

I turn around again and see Sofia on the ground. She's a couple of metres in front of a man who is also on the ground. When I was passing the gate, I noticed someone cleaning. I imagine that he had fallen over, having lost his balance like the others. What bad luck! Sofia has tripped over him. She is in pain on the ground.

"What's the matter? Are you OK?" Erik and I call out to her, running towards her to help her to her feet.

Sofia is crying. She has hurt her hand which is bleeding. Her face is bruised. She looks at us all and then looks backwards, as the first light of dawn appears. She shouts at us, with a mixture of hysteria and fear:

"Go ahead on your own. I can't"

CHAPTER 39

Friday 23 December 2016
Time: seconds before dawn

Sofia

Ay! What have I done to myself? I did not see the man who has just collapsed in front of me. I don't want to keep the group back. They have to succeed and I want them to continue. This cannot fail because of me. I would never forgive myself.

"We are not going to leave you here!" Erik shouts at me as he and David help me up.

Elsa and Samuel turn around to see what's happening.

"Forget me, you must go on ahead," I shout back insistently.

"Don't even think of it!" David says and turning to Erik, he suggests: "You have to open the portal with the music. Run! Go ahead of us, we'll follow with Sofia."

No one contradicts him because he's right. The time Erik needs to open the portal is the amount of time it will take for us to arrive... when I can run.

Erik sets off on a run, but before doing so, he bends over to kiss me. Samuel looks at me with tenderness and shows me his closed fist with the thumbs up sign. I manage to smile at him and try to sit up.

Elsa runs on ahead of us to ensure that there are no more obstacles ahead of us. I manage to stand and begin to run, but with a lot of pain. I can bear it. I *will* bear it.

In the distance, at the intersection, I see a man staring at us. The sun is almost reaching the intersection. Erik has just completed the last few metres remaining to get there and is taking out the dulzaina. David grabs my hand to help me and the two of us continue running. Suddenly, I touch my trousers. I have a hole in them after the fall. I continue to feel but I don't feel what I am looking for. I'm very nervous. As I'm running, holding on to David's hand, I turn to look back and there, in the distance, on the ground where I fell, I can make out the figure of the head of the god Janus that Nicola gave me last night. I cannot stop to get it! I continue running with a lot of pain, looking back. Darn it! I begin to feel fear when I notice that the man with whom I collided has picked it up and put it into his pocket. His face looks familiar. Suddenly, he smiles at me maliciously and I feel like vomiting. He is the guard at the museum who grabbed Elsa's arm and has been following us! What do I do? Oh, how painful this is!

"Come on! Come on!" David shouts at me to look ahead and run with him.

I forget the man. I focus once more on our objective. In the distance, I can see the weather vane of the building at the corner between Calle Mayor and Don Jaime Street. It is now completely bathed in sunlight. The light is reflected on its metallic colour which we've seen in recent days. We're not going to get there. I continue running, holding on to David's hand. I remember the man behind us, but I continue running straight ahead. I don't want to look back again.

Erik is ready with the dulzaina and shouts,

"Is it time yet?"

As we're not carrying anything, not even a watch, we cannot see. But at that moment, the first rays of sunshine light up the intersection and a shout in unison from the four of us can be heard throughout the intersection.

"Yes!"

Erik starts playing the music he had learnt by heart the night before. The rest of us stand around and look at him. A few passers-by stand still to observe us. Just as the music is coming to an end, there is a burst of light from the centre of the intersection and the wind picks up. As Erik continues playing, the lights get brighter and the wind gets stronger. He looks on as he plays. The others continue to observe the centre of the intersection. With a mixture of fear and admiration, we shift positions to prepare for the jump.

When Erik stops playing, in the very space between the streets, a portal opens up to the void, and without thinking, Elsa jumps in and disappears inside. Samuel follows with an agility that I've never seen before. Erik looks at me and also at David who signals to him to jump before me. David wants to wait behind to help me. Erik jumps quickly. When I'm about to do my jump, still holding on to David's hand, I feel a sharp stab of pain in my heart. Something has happened! I cannot control it. I look back and see David fainting and losing his balance.

"Noooo!" The sound escapes from the very depths of my soul as I try to reach him with my outstretched arm. I see him in the distance, collapsed on the ground, as I sink deep into the darkness.

Nature holds a great mystery, jealously guarded by its custodians from those who want to desecrate or abuse its wisdom.

From time to time, portions of its tradition are gradually revealed to the world of men, to those who have been attentive, with eyes to see and ears to hear.

The main requirement is a receptive mind, with the sensitivity, enthusiasm and responsibility to understand the deepest meaning of the marvels that nature shows us everyday.

Many of us tend to walk through life half asleep, sometimes paralysed or too clumsy to see the exquisite order that surrounds us. But a trail of clues has been preserved.

Scott Olsen
***The Golden Section* (2006)**

Glossary

Aragon: An autonomous community in north-eastern Spain, south of France. An autonomous community is similar to a state, as those in Australia or the United States, with its own administrative capital.

Augustus: Also known as Caesar Augustus, the first emperor of Rome. Born in 63 B.C. as Gaius Octavius, he was the great nephew of Julius Caesar who named him as his heir. On the death of his uncle, he founded the *Principate* which led to the creation of the Roman Empire, making himself the *Princeps Civitatis* or the 'First Citizen of the State', thereby becoming the first Roman Emperor. He conquered northern Spain in 19 B.C., and established the city of Caesaraugusta soon after.

Caesaraugusta: City founded by Caesar Augustus, and later called Zaragoza.

Calle Mayor: The Main Street.

Cierzo: A strong, dry and cold wind blowing from the North, over the North of Spain, specifically in the Ebro River valley, the autonomous regions of Aragon, Navarra, and La Rioja.

Dulzaina: This is a reed instrument of the Oboe family which is played throughout Spain. First introduced by the Arabs, it is widely played at festivals and used in traditional Spanish music.

Ebro: The Ebro River is the second longest river in Spain, with its source in Fontibre (from the Latin *Fontes Iberis,* which means *Source of the Ebro*) in the mountains in Cantabria, northern Spain. It flows eastwards across the north of the country through several cities, including Zaragoza, to empty into the Mediterranean Sea.

Fibonacci: Italian mathematician. Born Leonard Pisano Bonacci in Pisa (Italy) around 1175 A.D. and died around 1250 A.D., he became known as Fibonacci, derived from the Latin *Filius Bonacci* which means 'Son of Bonacci'. While living in

255

North Africa where his father worked as a customs officer, Fibonacci studied Arithmetic, using the Hindu-Arabic numbering system. It was Fibonacci who introduced the Hindu-Arabic numbers, which we use today, along with the decimal system to Europe. This replaced the Roman numerals which were used previously.

Mudéjar: An architectural and decorative style developed in Spain and Portugal, particularly in Aragon and Castile. It was influenced by mediaeval Islamic culture.

Paseo: Another word for street where, apart from cars running, there is always a middle part or "boulevard", with trees and benches for people to relax or have a stroll.

Plaza: A town square, providing areas for people to rest and relax. Some include trees and shrubs or other features like fountains. Town squares in European cities are sometimes used as marketplaces for itinerant market stalls once or twice a week.

Tapas: These are appetisers or snacks served in many Spanish bars to accompany drinks. They could be served hot or cold. Many restaurants and bars provide a *tapas* menu alongside a normal restaurant 'a la carte' menu.

Tortilla: The Spanish *tortilla* is an egg and potato omelette. It is a popular item on the *tapas* menu.

Zaragoza: The largest city and the administrative capital of Aragon, founded by Emperor Caesar Augustus, which he called *Caesaraugusta* after himself. This name was later changed to Zaragoza by the Arabs. It was formerly known in English as Saragossa.

BIBLIOGRAPHY

- The main idea for the story was inspired by the webpage of the Master Plan of the city of Zaragoza:

  o http://www.zaragoza.es/contenidos/medioambiente/Huerva/D5Analisis.pdf [accessed on 21.06.2014]. A lot of information and, in particular, all the street plans come from this source.

- The second idea for the story is based on:

  o **Cuartero, Raquel y Bolea, Chusé** (2014), Antiguas Puertas de Zaragoza [Ancient Gates of Zaragoza)] . Institución Fernando el Católico.

  o **Cantó, Alicia M.,** published work available on the Internet:

    ▪ http://www.academia.edu/1159116/La_Porta_Romana_y_los_Lares_de_Caesaraugusta [The Roman Gate and Guardian Gods of the Caesaraugusta] [accessed on 21.06.2014].

  o **Castán, María Pilar** (2013), La ciudad de Zaragoza, Nomenclátor, 1808 [The City of Zaragoza, Nomenclature, 1808]. Institución Fernando el Católico.

- Sacred Geometry:

  o **Olsen, Scott** (2009), The Golden Section. Wooden Books Ltd.

  o **Lawlor, Robert** (1982), Sacred Geometry: Philosophy & Practice. Thames & Hudson.

  o **Zatón, Jesús** (2015), GEOMETRÍA SAGRADA Bases naturales, científicas y pitagóricas (Sacred Geometry: Natural, Scientific and Pythagorean Foundations). Fundación Rosacruz.

- History:

  o **Hirst, John** (2009), The Shortest History of Europe. Old Street Publishing Ltd.

  o **Goldsworthy, Adrian** (2014), Augustus: From Revolutionary to Emperor. W&N (Weidenfeld & Nicolson)

www.ingramcontent.com/pod-product-compliance
Lightning Source LLC
Chambersburg PA
CBHW030822090426
42737CB00009B/831